MESSIANIC WISDOM

PRACTICAL
SCRIPTURAL ANSWERS
FOR YOUR LIFE
IN MESSIAH

BY
SAM NADLER

Messianic Wisdom
Practical Scriptural Answers
For Your Life in Messiah
by Sam Nadler
ISBN 13:978-1537640174/ISBN 10:1537640178
Printed in the United States of America
Copyright 2003© Sam Nadler/Word of Messiah Ministries
Third Printing 2016

Wisdom

Make your ear attentive to wisdom,
incline your heart to understanding.
Proverbs 2:2

The beginning of wisdom is:
Acquire wisdom;
and with all your acquiring,
get understanding.
Proverbs 4:7

Acquire wisdom!
Acquire understanding!
Do not forget nor turn away
from the words of my mouth.
Proverbs 4:5

Introduction

Shalom!

There are many challenging issues that face all Messianic believers in their spiritual walk. In this book are some biblical perspectives on these subjects.

In the Scriptures, God directs us to grow in wisdom. Wisdom itself is defined as "understanding what is right, true, and lasting...a wise outlook or course of action."[1] It is the skill for living, the application of knowledge.

The beginning of godly wisdom is a proper, reverent attitude towards the Lord.[2] This reverent attitude is demonstrated by accepting and applying God's perspective in our daily lives.

I trust that as you search out God's Word you will indeed gain "Messianic wisdom," since *"the sacred writings...are able to give you the wisdom that leads to salvation through faith which is in Messiah Yeshua."*[3]

Just as Yeshua *"became to us wisdom from God,"*[4] may He lead you to live in such a way that He will be glorified in your life!

For Yeshua's Glory,

Sam Nadler

---

[1] The American Heritage College Dictionary, Third Edition; [2] See Psalm 111:10, Proverbs 9:10; [3] 2 Timothy 3:15; [4] 1 Corinthians 1:30

ACKNOWLEDGEMENTS

I want to thank some people whose insights and wisdom I have drawn from throughout my life as a believer.

A friend named 'Whit', whose practical counseling is a blessing to many. He has been a source of encouragement and insight to me through the years.

Dr. Louis Goldberg, former professor of Jewish Studies at Moody Bible College. Dr. Goldberg's encouragement to me in his final two years on this side of heaven was invaluable, like refined gold.

Two of Dr. Goldberg's students, Dr. Michael Rydelnik, professor of Jewish Studies at Moody Bible College, and Howard Silverman, the Congregation Leader at *Beth Messiah* in Columbus, Ohio, are friends that have generously shared their knowledge and wisdom with me.

My wife Miriam, who has been a constant source of sensitivity and insight, especially regarding relationship and emotional issues that impact people's spiritual lives: her suggestions, additions and deletions were invaluable.

Special thanks to Pat Campbell for all his help and for designing the cover of this book.

To these and many others I say, "Thank you."

Sam Nadler

Table of Contents

Introduction 5

1. Messianic Jewish Identity 13

2. Gentiles in the spiritual Family 30

3. Torah and The Messianic Believer 45

4. Considering Synagogues, Churches, and Messianic Congregations 64

5. Finding a Good Congregation 78

6. Confessing the Faith...Wisely 85

7. Messianic Marriage and Dating 94

8. Messianic Believers and Circumcision .. 116

9. Messianic Believers and Bar/Bat Mitzvah 123

10. Celebrating Biblical and Jewish Holidays 138

11. Celebrating "Christian" Holidays..........145

12. Your Testimony at Home......................158

13. Dealing with Death in the Family......164

14. Your Faith and Your Finances.............175

Appendix
A Messianic Statement of Faith.................187

Charts
   Prophecies of the Messiah.......................193
   Redemption in the Feasts of Israel........194

Shabbat Blessings for Your Home.............196

Do's and Don'ts When Sharing..................198

A Simple Prayer of Faith.............................199

Other Books & Materials by WMM........200

Additional Helpful Resources.....................201

Messianic Wisdom

Practical Scriptural Answers For Your Life in Messiah

By
Sam Nadler

CHAPTER ONE

MESSIANIC JEWISH IDENTITY

FOR YOU ARE A HOLY PEOPLE
TO THE LORD YOUR GOD;
THE LORD YOUR GOD HAS CHOSEN YOU
TO BE A PEOPLE FOR HIS OWN POSSESSION
OUT OF ALL THE PEOPLES WHO ARE
ON THE FACE OF THE EARTH...
...BECAUSE THE LORD LOVED YOU
AND KEPT THE OATH WHICH HE SWORE
TO YOUR FOREFATHERS.
— MOSES
DEUTERONOMY 7:6-8A

I SAY THEN,
HAS GOD CAST AWAY HIS PEOPLE?
CERTAINLY NOT!
FOR I ALSO AM AN ISRAELITE,
OF THE SEED OF ABRAHAM,
OF THE TRIBE OF BENJAMIN.
GOD HAS NOT CAST AWAY HIS PEOPLE
WHOM HE FOREKNEW.
— RABBI SHAUL (PAUL)
ROMANS 11:1,2

If you are Jewish, it is critical that you understand your identity as a Jewish believer in Messiah. There are some who would say that because you believe in Yeshua you are no longer a Jew. How do you respond to such a false accusation? More importantly, how are you to grapple with the issue of your Jewish identity? That is, how do you have integrity in your identity both as a believer in Yeshua, and as a Jewish person?

If you are not Jewish, keep reading. This chapter will be very helpful for you in your study of the issue of Jewish identity. Understanding these biblical issues will enable you to encourage others, and to communicate more effectively to Jewish people the validity of the Scriptural facts about Yeshua.

WHAT IS A MESSIANIC BELIEVER?

The word *Messiah* is the exact equivalent of the word *Christ*. The Hebrew word *Mashiach*, which means "Anointed One," is transliterated into English as *Messiah*. When *Mashiach* is translated into the Greek, the word is *Christos*, which transliterated into English is *Christ*. Though the words Messiah and Christ, as well as the adjectives *messianic* and *christian*, are technically equivalent, over the years they have acquired some additional cultural connotations, and are many times misunderstood.

To many people Christ is the central Person of the Christian faith, but Messiah is the hope of the Jewish people. So also with the label

"Christian." Generally, to Jewish people the word Christian means non-Jew. Therefore when a Jewish person becomes a believer in Yeshua, to call him or her a Christian indicates to the Jewish community that this person has deserted the Jewish people, and 'joined the Gentiles'. A Jewish person who becomes a Christian is now considered by the Jewish community, for all intents and purposes to be a non-Jew. In order to prevent any misunderstanding of our faith by the Jewish community, we Jewish believers—and those in fellowship with Jewish believers—have come to use the term "Messianic believer" to describe ourselves. Jewish believers are still Jews, because Yeshua *is* the Jewish Messiah, as well as Savior of the world.

IT'S A JEWISH THING

Regarding the Jewish identity of Jewish believers, the real issue is Yeshua. If He is the true Jewish Messiah, then a Jewish person who places faith in Him has made the most Jewish act of faith that he or she could ever do! Indeed, it's a *mitzvah* (the fulfillment of a commandment), since God has called all Jews and all Gentiles to believe in Messiah Yeshua—*"Go make disciples of all nations."*[1] From the very first words of Matthew's account, the New Covenant declares Yeshua to be the Jewish Messiah :

"The record of the genealogy of Yeshua the Messiah, the son of David, the son of Abraham."[2]

As the Good News *according to Matthew* was written for a Jewish audience, the Good

News *according to John* was written for a Gentile audience. Even when John (*Yochanan* in Hebrew) wrote to Gentiles, He presented Yeshua for who He is: the long-awaited *Jewish* Messiah. Notice the terms John uses in John 1:29-49...

> *"Behold the **Lamb of God** who takes away the sin of the world! And I myself have seen and have testified that this is the **Son of God**..." "Look, here is the **Lamb of God**!..." "They [the disciples] said to him, **'Rabbi'**..."We have found the **Messiah**..." "We have found him about whom **Moses in the Law** and also the prophets wrote, Yeshua from Nazareth..." "**Rabbi**, you are the **Son of God**! You are the **King of Israel**!"*

There isn't one *non*-Jewish description of Yeshua in the Bible, because there was, and is, nothing *non*-Jewish about Him. He is always presented as the Jewish Messiah. In fact, compared to the modern Western understanding of Yeshua, John wrote of Him in what might be considered an unusual fashion:

> *And Yeshua turned and saw them following, and said to them, "What do you seek?" They said to Him, "Rabbi (which translated means Teacher), where are You staying?"...He found first his own brother Simon and said to him, "We have found the Messiah" (which translated means Christ). He brought him to Yeshua. Yeshua looked at him and said, "You are Simon the son of John; you shall be called Cephas" (which is translated Peter)* (John 1:38,41,42).

Notice that in each of these verses John writes the Hebrew words *Rabbi, Messiah* and *Cephas*, then follows them with the Greek translations, *Teacher, Christ* and *Peter*.

Why did John do this? Because even as Matthew was writing his biography of Yeshua to a Jewish audience, so John was writing his account of Messiah to a Greek speaking audience. It is unlikely that a Greek audience would understand the Hebrew terms he used, therefore John was careful to translate so Greeks could appreciate what was being taught.

MESSIAH & SAVIOR

That's all well and good, but if you're just going to have to translate it anyway, why bother stating the Hebrew words at all? Consider this: since *all Scripture is inspired by God and profitable*[3], and since John was especially careful to include only necessary information[4], we know that there was a reason John wrote this way. When John wrote to the Gentile world about the essential need for faith in Yeshua, he dared not separate Messiah from His biblical *and* Jewish roots. Though his Gospel account would declare Yeshua to be the Savior of the world[5], Yeshua's credentials for being the *world's* Savior rely upon His being *Israel's* true Messiah. If Yeshua is not the rightful Jewish Messiah He has no authority to be anyone's savior, let alone the Savior of the world. The only way Gentiles could hope in Jesus as their Savior is if they understood that He is the authentic Jewish Messiah. To separate Him from His Jewish roots is to separate Messiah from His legitimate, eternal authority and ministry. *Gentiles must remain aware of these Jewish roots of the faith.*

Lest We Forget

The congregation at Rome had forgotten the Jewish roots of their faith, and the Gentile believers there had become arrogant towards Jewish people and Old Covenant teaching. Eventually they came to believe that they supported the root [Israel] when in fact the root supported them[6]! The same mistake can, and does happen today.

In the first century, Jewish people who came to believe in Yeshua *never* thought of themselves as anything but Jewish. For instance, in Acts 21:39 Paul replied, *"I am a Jew, from Tarsus in Cilicia..."* and in Acts 22:3, *"I am a Jew, born in Tarsus of Cilicia."* In Romans 11:1 Paul writes, *"I ask, then, has God rejected his people? By no means! For I am an Israelite, a descendant of Abraham, of the tribe of Benjamin."*

Because Paul was sent to preach Messiah to the Gentiles, some people may think that he had given up being Jewish. Not at all. The New Covenant has never taught that Jews should stop being Jews and "become" Gentiles. On the contrary, the New Covenant reinforces the Jewish believer's Jewish identity in Messiah!

Genuine or Counterfeit?

Throughout history there have been anti-Semites who have called themselves 'Christians'. Tragically, this has given Messiah a bad name among Jewish people who are unaware of the biblical facts, and caused most of them to think that believing in Yeshua as Messiah is the most 'non-Jewish' thing a Jew could ever do. Though Messiah's Name has been discredited by many anti-Semites perpetrating their evil deeds under a religious guise, this in no way makes a Jew 'no-longer-a-Jew' simply because of their faith in the Biblical Jesus. Rather, the question that should be asked is, "Were those Gentiles truly authentic believers in Yeshua?" How can a so-called 'Christian' say he has the 'King of the Jews' living in his heart, and at the same time hate Jewish people? The fact of the matter is, Messiah Himself has warned us that such people would come. So it should be no surprise when false prophets, false teachers, "wolves in sheep's clothing" do come. This actually confirms the truth of His word.[7]

EAT AT MO'S

Below we see an illustration of the misunderstanding many have about Jewish believers in Messiah.[*]

> It is true that at this present time the majority of believers in Yeshua are non-Jews. But that doesn't change the fact that Yeshua is still the true Jewish Messiah and that faith in Him does not, and cannot, make Jews into Gentiles. Allow me to illustrate this idea with a story. It's about a Jewish restaurant (the Bible), the food it served (Yeshua, the 'bread of life'- [see John 6:35]), and the mostly Gentile neighborhood (the world) where the restaurant was located. If this Jewish restaurant served such great food that so many Gentiles became patrons of the restaurant, would that make the food non-Jewish? Of course not! Jews could still eat there and enjoy the 'home cooking'.
> And if those same Gentile patrons enjoyed the food so

[*]Excerpted from this author's book *"Growing in Messiah"*

much that they took some home in their own non-Jewish containers (so everyone mistakenly thought that the food came from a non-Jewish restaurant), that still wouldn't change one fact about the food, or the restaurant, being Jewish! How ridiculous to think that Jews who eat in that restaurant stop being Jewish.

The irony is this: at first, and quite a while ago, some of the Jewish patrons thought that any Gentile patrons of such a Jewish restaurant had to become Jewish! In fact, it became a real controversy for the Jewish restaurant. So much so, that all the original Jewish patrons came together to discuss this issue. It was finally decided that "Gentiles that eat Jewish food don't become Jewish, just fulfilled Gentiles!"
(You can read of the actual controversy and decision in Acts 15.)

Let's say for argument's sake, that Yeshua *is* a false Messiah. Still, even as a believer in Yeshua I must be seen as a Jew in the eyes of rabbinical authority. Why? Because, believing in a 'false Messiah' does not make any Jew a non-Jew. For example, during the Jewish revolt against Rome (132 A.D./C.E), Rabbi Akiba (a very famous Rabbi) declared Simon Bar Cochba, leader of the revolt, to be the Messiah, although he had none of the acknowledged messianic credentials! It appeared to be merely Akiba's pragmatic attempt to unite all Jews against Rome. Since that time, however, no Jewish authority has ever said, "Akiba is no longer Jewish for believing in a false Messiah." If Akiba is still 'a Jew in good standing', then a Jew who believes in Yeshua as the Messiah, cannot be considered otherwise.[8]

And remember, just because you are still Jewish does not mean you are better or closer to God than anyone else. There was never anything about being Jewish that made us better than Gentiles. You may find that some well-meaning Gentile believers may treat you like a celebrity for believing in Yeshua. Please, "don't believe your press." Remind them that though you are Jewish, you are not necessarily a *maven*, an expert or 'know-it-all', on all things Jewish, nor an expert on the Tanakh (Old Covenant). In fact, you have just as much need for discipleship in the things of God as anyone—maybe more! Paul declared, *"There dwells no good thing in my flesh"*[9] and *"All have sinned and fall short of the glory of God."*[10] By "All" he is referring to both Jews and Gentiles.

THE CHOSEN PEOPLE

Being the "Chosen People"[11] was not meant to speak of Jewish physical or spiritual qualities, but of God's demonstration of mercy upon a people that would not exist if not for His divine mercy. Even as the Scriptures declare:

> *The LORD did not set His love on you nor choose you because you were more in number than any other people, for you were the least of all peoples; but because the LORD loves you, and because He would keep the oath which He swore to your fathers...* (Deut. 7:7,8).

> *Therefore understand that the LORD your God is not giving you this good land to possess because of your righteousness, for you are a stubborn people* (Deut. 9:6).

> *"Behold, the days are coming," says the LORD, "that I will punish all who are circumcised with the uncircumcised -- Egypt, Judah, Edom, the people of Ammon, Moab, and all who are in the farthest corners, who dwell in the wilderness. For all these nations are uncircumcised, and all the house of Israel are uncircumcised in the heart"* (Jeremiah 9:24,25).

Notice that in none of these portions is there any statement regarding the greatness of our people—not that we are all that bad either, mind you. As people go we're as good as any, but that's not the point. The point is that God chose Israel, not because of any intrinsic spiritual prominence as a people, but that Israel would glorify God, Who is truly great. Life is not all about Israel, but it is all about God. Even as the frame is to focus attention on the picture, so Israel is the frame; God is the picture.

Therefore Jewish people exist by God's mercy which is demonstrated in the promises He made to Abraham,[12] and reiterated in the prophets, such as in Jeremiah:

> *Thus says the LORD, who gives the sun for light by day and the fixed order of the moon and the stars for light by night, who stirs up the sea so that its waves roar-- the LORD of hosts is his name: If this fixed order were ever to cease from my presence, says the LORD, then also the offspring of Israel would cease to be a nation before me forever. Thus says the LORD: If the heavens above can be measured, and the foundations of the earth below can be explored, then I will reject all the offspring of Israel because of all they have done, says the LORD*
> (Jeremiah 31:35-37).

Jeremiah writes that the cosmos will have to be changed before Israel ceases to exist as a people before the Lord. It is God's will that we maintain our identity as Jews, for we therefore demonstrate that faith in Yeshua does not hinder our existence as Jews, but rather that He is the very Hope of Israel. God will keep our people, and Jewish believers are living proof that His promises are not rescinded in Yeshua, but are reinforced in Him. Our boast is to be in the Lord.

> But by His doing you are in Messiah Yeshua, who became to us wisdom from God, and righteousness and sanctification, and redemption, so that, just as it is written, "Let him who boasts, boast in the Lord" (1 Cor. 1:30,31).

Our Jewish identity is a fact just like being male or female. It's nothing in itself to be proud of or ashamed of, but simply a fact that doesn't change upon coming to faith in Yeshua.

Shimon, an Israeli believer, met with me shortly after he had come to faith in Messiah Yeshua. He was curious about this "Jewish identity" issue. Since he only wanted to glorify Jesus and not put any trust in the flesh, this Jewish issue seemed to him to be no more than fleshly pride. After studying the Scriptures together, he saw that it was no more prideful to be identified as a Jewish believer than to be a male believer, it was just the facts of the matter. In fact, according to Scripture, to identify as a Jewish believer in Messiah was now a matter of testifying to God's faithfulness to His promises, even as Paul did in Romans 11:1,2. Shimon has matured as a Jewish believer, and though he still wants to be careful that he puts no trust in his flesh, he is also bold to declare, *"Am Yisrael Chai BaShem Yeshua HaMashiach!"* That is, *"The People of Israel live in the name of Yeshua the Messiah!"*

OY! HOW THEN DO I LIVE?

The question may come up, "But how do I live as a Jew?" As we survey the worldwide Jewish community we see there are many different Jewish lifestyles. Some Jews are more orthodox in their Jewish expression, and some are less, but all are considered by the Jewish community at large to be valid Jewish lifestyles. The scenario is the same with Messianic Jewish believers. Some choose to live a more orthodox lifestyle, while others are quite content to maintain a significantly less orthodox expression. As Paul taught, *"Let each person be fully convinced in his own mind."*[13]

WHO REALLY CARES?

Some might wonder why a Messianic Jew would be concerned with what the Jewish community thinks about his Jewish identity. But we do care, and for two very good reasons. We identify with our Jewish people that we may effectively communicate the Good News. Even more importantly, we live as Jews to demonstrate the faithfulness of God to our people:

> Hath God cast away his people? God forbid. For I also am an Israelite, of the seed of Abraham, of the tribe of Benjamin. God hath not cast away his people which he foreknew.[14]

In review, we noted the use of "Messianic" as a label or an adjective. Jewish believers in Yeshua who identify with their Jewish roots of faith, and their Jewish culture as an expression of their faith, are called *Messianic Jews*. Gentile believers who identify with the Jewish roots of the faith, and Jewish culture as an expression of their faith, are called *Messianic Gentiles*. Both may be called *Messianic believers*.

WHAT ABOUT THEIR CHILDREN?

Jews are Jews by birth. According to traditional Judaism, it's the mother's Jewishness that counts, but according to the Bible, *either* parent will suffice. For instance, Joseph's Egyptian wife didn't prevent his children, Ephraim and Manasseh, from being considered bona fide *children of Israel*, as Jews were called at that particular time in history.[15] Similarly, Gentiles are Gentiles by birth, and both Jews and Gentiles become believers by faith in Yeshua.

The children of believing Jewish parents are Jews, but not yet believers. Children must come to faith in Yeshua for themselves in order to be saved and become regenerated children of God. Likewise, children of believing Gentile parents are Gentiles and not believers, unless they too come to personal faith in Yeshua. As it's been said before, being born in a bakery doesn't make you a bagel! Jews are not Jews by faith, but by birth. Gentiles are not Gentiles by unbelief, but by birth. A personal relationship with God is not based on being Jewish, and is not negated by being Gentile—but through faith in Yeshua. Period.

CHRISTIAN? JEW?

Some Jewish believers do not identify with the Jewish roots of their faith, or with the Jewish culture as an expression of their faith in Messiah. They prefer rather to identify with a Gentile culture to express their faith.

They are comfortable being called Christian Jews, Jewish Christians, or Hebrew Christians. These are valid terms, but often such Jewish believers have no connection at all to their Jewish background or identity, and feel quite comfortable just being called Christians. Some may even feel uncomfortable being called "Jewish" without the term Christian attached, like they are in some way evading or even denying their faith.

THE NEXT GENERATION

Jewish believers who prefer to be identified as Christians or Hebrew Christians are certainly still Jews. But they risk becoming less effective in the communication of their testimony by being culturally irrelevant to the Jewish community, and in many cases even to their own family. Their children may eventually be found saying, "Yes, my mother was Jewish, but I'm not." Or "I'm part-Jewish, or "half-Jewish." Eventually it may be heard, "I think my grandfather was Jewish." Often these children can lack a personal bond with their own Jewish identity. This issue of Messianic testimony requires careful, thoughtful consideration by every Jewish believer.

These Jewish believers are greatly encouraged to be very careful that they do not essentially end the existence of the Jewish people in their own family line. This can be fraught with difficulties.

There may be Jewish believers in locales that do not have a sound Messianic congregation, and the only sound teaching for the family is in a church with a Gentile culture. In attempting to give their children some kind of Jewish identity, the Jewish believer in a church may appear to some to over emphasize his own Jewish identity. At times this can cause confusion for Gentile members of the church, who may wrongly interpret a lack of 'cultural uniformity' as a lack of spiritual unity. Unfortunately, they may perceive the Messianic believer's Jewish heritage as prideful, or even divisive.

Also, when Messianic parents are committed to maintaining a Jewish identity in a Gentile-cultured church, at times the Jewish children feel like they are "different" and "stick out." They're "Jewish," but the other kids are just "Christians." In a Gentile church it's not easy to maintain Jewish identity. But since when has it ever been easy to be a Jew?!

Though we are responsible to identify as Jews, we have liberty in our personal expression of our Jewishness. May this freedom in Messiah give you greater opportunity to encourage others in the faith, share Messiah with those who do not yet know Him, and further glorify the Lord each day as you wisely walk by faith through life!

QUESTIONS
For Your Further Study and Consideration

Why did God choose the Jewish People, and why does He desire to keep us as an identifiable people?
(see Jeremiah 31:35-37; Romans 11:1-6)

Are there any more blessings for a Jewish believer than for a Gentile believer, or in being a male believer than a female believer? Why or why not?
(See Ephesians 1:3; Colossians 2:9,10; Gal. 3:28)

As a Jew, in what way can I live so as to retain the Jewishness of my testimony in Messiah?
(See Colossians 2:16-17; Romans 14:1-9)

How can I raise my children to appreciate their identity, responsibility and liberty as a Jewish believer? (May they come to faith early in life!)

FOOTNOTES
[1] Matthew 28:19
[2] Matthew 1:1
[3] 2 Timothy 3:16
[4] John 20:30,31; 21:25
[5] John 4:42
[6] see Romans 11:18
[7] see Matthew 7:15
[8] Excerpted from WMM's *"The Messianic Answer Book"*
[9] Romans 7:18
[10] Romans 3:23
[11] See Deut. 7:6
[12] Genesis 12:2,3
[13] Rom. 14:5
[14] Romans 11:1,2
[15] Genesis 41:45-52, see also Ruth 4:10-22

Chapter Two

Gentiles in the Spiritual Family

I WILL ALSO MAKE YOU [MESSIAH] A LIGHT OF
THE NATIONS [GENTILES] SO THAT MY SALVATION
MAY REACH TO THE END OF THE EARTH. — GOD
ISAIAH 49:6

ALL NATIONS WHOM THOU HAST MADE
SHALL COME AND WORSHIP BEFORE THEE,
O LORD; AND THEY SHALL GLORIFY THY NAME.
— DAVID
PSALM 86:9

If you were not born Jewish and believe in Yeshua, you are a "messianic Gentile." *Mazel Tov*[1], and welcome to the family! That being said, just as there are misconceptions about Jewish believers, there are as well some misconceptions about Gentile believers in Messiah that need to be clarified.

The Issue of the Messianic Gentile.

First, what is a "Gentile?" The word *gentile* simply means *"one of the nations"*, and is derived from the Latin *gens* meaning "nation."

This is a direct parallel to the Hebrew word for nation, *goy* (plural, "*goyim*"). Unfortunately, just as anti-Semites use the word Jew in a negative manner, the word gentile or goy is often mistakenly thought of as a synonym for "pagan/anti-Semite/christian."

WHY WOULD THERE BE ANY BIBLICAL USAGE OF THE TERM "GENTILE" EQUATING TO "PAGAN?"

Before Yeshua came and was proclaimed among the nations, the customary way for Gentiles to 'get right with God' was to become a proselyte, or convert, to Judaism. All non-Jews at that time were considered pagans since they were not permitted into the Temple to make the appropriate sacrifice for his or her sins. Therefore in Matthew's account Yeshua said,

> *And when you are praying, do not use meaningless repetition as the Gentiles do, for they suppose that they will be heard for their many words (*Matthew 6:7*).*
>
> *If he refuses to listen to them, tell it to the church; and if he refuses to listen even to the church, let him be to you as a Gentile and a tax collector* (Matthew 18:17).

Yeshua's disciples at the time of His earthly ministry were all Jews, and as such, they believed that the religion of truth was the Jewish religion. They lived in a traditional Jewish frame of reference and Gentiles, by definition, were not part of 'the people of God', and were considered outside of the Jewish religion.[2]

Today however, because of the apostasy of traditional Judaism, it is more accurate to call our Messianic faith '*biblical* faith', rather than 'the *Jewish* faith'.

Though conversion to Judaism was at one time the only way for Gentiles to be accepted in the Biblical faith, Yeshua 'hints' at the inclusion of the Gentiles into the people of God[3]—but only a hint. For Yeshua at that time to clearly mention Gentiles as co-heirs with Jews would have been distracting to His disciples. Since at the time many people identified Gentiles with paganism, this truth regarding Gentiles to be accepted as co-heirs *with Jewish believers* in Yeshua, and *yet remaining as non-Jews*, awaited further and future revelation.

ARE GENTILES STILL GENTILES AFTER COMING TO FAITH IN MESSIAH YESHUA?

When Paul was writing to the congregation in Rome, he addressed the non-Jewish believers there by saying, *"But I am speaking to you who are Gentiles."*[4] Just as Paul referred to himself in Acts 22:3 and in Romans 11:1 in the *present tense* as a "Jew" and as an "Israelite", so he now refers to the non-Jewish believers in the present tense as "Gentiles." In other words, though they are saved and brethren in the faith[5], they are *still* Gentiles, that is, non-Jews, and it's okay.

In Messiah, Gentiles are truly co-heirs with Jewish believers, but this does not mean either group loses its personal identity. Read Galatians 3:28 carefully—*"There is neither Jew nor Greek, there is neither bond nor free, there is neither male nor female: for ye are all one in Messiah Yeshua."*

Faith in Yeshua does not change a person's cultural, national or ethnic identity any more than faith would change their gender or the color of their skin. As surely as Jews remain Jews when they come to faith in Yeshua,[6] so also do Gentiles remain Gentiles after coming to faith in Yeshua.

This is good news: God loves diversity. Of course He does—He created it, and has redeemed it! Our unity is not experienced through uniformity, and our diversity does not necessarily bring division. The reality of our unity is based upon the truth of who Yeshua is and what He has actually done for all who believe in Him. This reality of our unity in Yeshua is experienced as we live out our faith in Him and love one another. Our diversity with unity brings greater glory to God as His life is manifested trans-culturally and trans-ethnically.[7]

This unity with diversity demonstrates grace and love through Yeshua as the spiritual way and witness of peace and harmony in the world—

A new commandment I give unto you, that ye love one another; as I have loved you, that ye also love one another. By this shall all men know that ye are my disciples, if ye have love one to another (John 13:34,35).

A NEW WINESKIN

Once the body of Messiah was miraculously birthed by *Ruach HaKodesh* (the Holy Spirit) at Pentecost[8], a new work was underway and a new "wineskin"[9] was developed—Gentiles could come into the faith without converting to Judaism! But it took a number of years for this to happen, and even more years for Gentiles to be fully accepted by all. In fact, just to get an apostle to accept a Gentile took a revelation from God. Yes, it took a divine revelation from God to get Peter to even visit a Gentile home in order to preach the Good News![10] Even then the other leaders called Peter "on the carpet" for daring to associate with a Gentile—and Peter was the first leader among the early believers![11]

When Gentiles came to faith in large numbers in Antioch, it was such a questionable situation that the matter had to be officially investigated.[12] Even years later when Paul preached that Gentile believers were a part of the body of Messiah— without their needing to get circumcised—it caused quite a theological controvesy.[13] Finally, on that occasion it was officially determined that it was spiritually O.K. for Gentile believers in Messiah to remain Gentiles. It was, and is, by grace that they were saved, not by becoming Jewish or by any works of Torah![14] Despite this apostolic decision, I'm sure that the anti-Gentile prejudice lasted for years[15] and provided no small amount of tension and disagreement. This tension may have contributed to a reaction by the Roman Gentile believers, and their arrogance against the Jewish people.[16]

The Biblical faith had been so closely identified with the Jewish people for so long, that it was revolutionary to separate the Biblical faith from the Jewish culture.

Gentiles had been so identified with pagan religion that it seemed heretical to allow them to remain gentile in their identity as a people group after coming to faith in Messiah. But the revelation of God has now been fully given, and salvation—an eternal relationship with God—is based on faith in Yeshua alone: not in being Jewish, or non-Jewish.[17] The true faith was to be seen as something purely spiritual without any particular national or cultural affiliation, even as Yeshua alluded.[18] The biblical faith was now going to be relevant to all and proclaimed to all people and nations. Later, Paul would articulate the revelation of this new spiritual reality, by saying that Jews and Gentiles are equals and co-heirs in the Body of Messiah.[19] We are spiritually the same, and fully accepted in the sight of God!

All this being said, today there are still some people who confuse Gentile with pagan, even as there are some who think Jew equates to "non-believer in Yeshua." Gentile doesn't mean pagan any more than Jew means non-believer in Yeshua. Though people have abused both the words Jew and Gentile (or Goy) there is nothing inherently wrong with either of these biblical terms.

CAN JEWISH & GENTILE BELIEVERS HAVE REAL UNITY WITHOUT GENTILES BECOMING JEWS?

Yes, we can. The revelation of true spiritual unity is that all believers in Yeshua are *one body* in the sight of God.[20] The fact that the Body of Messiah is made up of Jews and Gentiles is no more a problem than its being made up of men and women, or black and white people. The problem is, many confuse unity with uniformity. Webster defines *unity* as *oneness, a condition of harmony*. However, *uniformity* is defined as *having at all times the same form, manner or degree; presenting an undiversified appearance*. But can there be unity without uniformity? Is it only when we all 'look, sound, and dress alike' that we will then be in unity? Such is not the teaching of Scripture.

UNITY OF THE SPIRIT

The New Covenant truth is that our unity is based on our personal relationship with Yeshua Himself, and not in mere cultural or ethnic appearance. This is the hope of Psalm 133:1.

> Behold, how good and how pleasant it is for brothers to dwell together in unity!

So also is Yeshua's prayer in John 17:20-23...

> I do not ask on behalf of these alone, but for those also who believe in Me through their word; that they may all be one; even as You, Father, are in Me and I in You, that they also may be in Us, so that the world may believe that You sent Me. The glory which You have given Me I have given to them, that they may be one, just as We are one; I in them and You in Me, that they may be perfected in unity, so that the world may know that You sent Me, and loved them, even as You have loved Me.

Our unity is spiritual, rather than cultural; it is made genuine in Messiah, rather than through customs; and it is preserved through our diligence,[21] rather than by rituals. This unity is the true goal of the body of Messiah.[22]

Therefore, whether in a Christian church or a Messianic congregation, there is no assurance of unity just because people participate in the same rituals and customs—that would be uniformity, rather than unity. Only as we express faith in Yeshua through love of the brethren are we expressing true spiritual unity, regardless of the cultural format.

Some may think that diversity of expression leads to division of faith. The disciples of Yeshua thought so as well and had to be corrected by Messiah.[23] Remember, unity does not mean Jews become Gentiles, or Gentiles become Jews. To teach such a loss of personal identity would actually hurt the true work of Messiah. It is not being Jewish or Gentile that is the spiritual problem; the true spiritual problem that Messiah totally and effectively dealt with is sin. To place the focus of a "conversion" on anything other than "turning *from sin*," is to say that the real issue Messiah came to deal with is racial or cultural—and this is just plain wrong. So, it's okay to be blond-haired and blue-eyed, or have dark hair, eyes and skin, or to be red-headed with freckles! By faith in Yeshua we are all in one spiritual family, and therefore we are to accept one another just as He has accepted each of us.[24]

Still some might say, "But didn't Messiah come so that *in Himself He might make the two into one new man*?" Indeed, he did, but in so doing, it was as though He took lead and silver and wanted to make it one new metal. The lead might say, "the silver must become lead."

The silver would say, "the lead must become silver." But the Master turned them both into something greater than either one—gold! In our unity the whole is greater than the sum of its parts.

THE BLESSING OF ABRAHAM

Though we are diverse in our identity as Jewish and Gentile believers, we are all children of Abraham by faith in Yeshua the Messiah, even as the New Covenant teaches so clearly:

> *For this reason it is by faith, in order that it may be in accordance with grace, so that the promise will be guaranteed to all the descendants, not only to those who are of the Law, but also to those who are of the faith of Abraham, who is the father of us all, (as it is written, "a father of many nations have I made you")* (Rom. 4: 16,17).
>
> *Therefore, be sure that it is those who are of faith who are sons of Abraham. The Scripture, foreseeing that God would justify the Gentiles by faith, preached the gospel beforehand to Abraham, saying, "all the nations will be blessed in you." So then those who are of faith are blessed with Abraham, the believer...in order that in Messiah Yeshua the blessing of Abraham might come to the Gentiles, so that we would receive the promise of the Spirit through faith* (Gal. 4:7–9,14).

Therefore by faith in Yeshua, Jews don't become spiritual Gentiles, but spiritual Jews; and by faith in Yeshua, Gentiles don't become spiritual Jews but spiritual Gentiles. All become brothers and sisters by faith in Messiah, and all the blessings that God has for each person are in Messiah Yeshua,[25] and not in being Jewish or Gentile. Spiritually, the flesh profits nothing, regardless of whose flesh it may be.

By way of illustration, in the United States George Washington is considered to be the "father of our country." As citizens of the United States, we might call ourselves "sons of Washington" as long as we hold to the same democratic ideals. Similarly, we may call ourselves sons of Abraham as long as we hold to the same faith ideals of Abraham, *"the father of us all."* [26]

SHOULD GENTILES 'CONVERT' TO BECOME JEWISH OR MESSIANIC JEWS?

In light of the full atonement and complete acceptance in Messiah Yeshua for everyone who believes in Him, not only is it unnecessary to convert, but it is wrong. To convert to Judaism *after* coming to faith in Messiah is an affront to the very Good News itself! If what Yeshua did for us is not enough to complete us in God's sight, then nothing will ever satisfy God's righteous judgment, or our souls. We are not to look to the flesh, national identity, or our ethnic background as fulfillment of our lives, or to achieve some special status with God. We are complete in Messiah.[27]

CONVERTING TO TRADITIONAL JUDAISM

Though this may sound stern, it must be said without ambiguity or apology: any truly born again Gentile believer who converts to traditional Judaism is terribly confused and spiritually deceived. Traditional Judaism is plainly and simply a false religion, as is any religion that denies Yeshua as Messiah, Savior, and God.

To willingly convert to another religion from true biblical faith is denying the very basis of that faith. In reality, such a person has gone *apostate* and placed himself under the wrath of God for despising the blood of Yeshua as sufficient for a right relationship with God.[28] Obviously, this is a very serious issue, and unless there is repentance it is questionable whether the person was ever a believer at all.[29]

Some Gentile believers may consider converting to traditional Judaism—without giving up their faith in Messiah—perhaps in the hope of witnessing more effectively to the Jewish people. To do so indicates a lack of understanding of the issues, and perhaps even a lack of integrity. One needs to realize that to convert to Judaism is to agree with the viewpoint that Yeshua is *not* the Messiah. Additionally, a certain level of integrity is rightly expected by the Jewish community. They would expect that the person is converting with a sincere heart and not with a hidden agenda.

Though we should respect people of other faiths—just as we would want them to respect us—we should not think that a non-biblical faith is true, or acceptable to God. Not at all. Yeshua is God's only way of bringing humanity to Himself. All false religions are recognized by their answer to the question, "Who is Yeshua?" Anything less than "God,"[30] *"the only mediator between God and man,"*[31] and the only way to the Father,[32] defines these belief systems as false,[33] no matter how sincere the individuals involved may be.

Converting to "Messianic Judaism"

There are some Messianic leaders and congregations that have "converted" Gentile believers into becoming Messianic Jews. So, if you were to ask them, "Are you a Gentile?" They would presumably be able to say, "No, I'm a Messianic Jew."

Any Gentile believer that "converts" to Messianic Judaism is following non-biblical and strange teaching. Such teaching denies the truth that all of God's blessings are in Yeshua *alone*: *"Blessed be the God and Father of our Lord Yeshua the Messiah, who has blessed us with **every spiritual blessing** in the heavenly places **in Messiah**."*[34] We are to find contentment in the Lord and enjoy our relationship with God. Such conversion teaching focuses on placing one's faith in the flesh and personal performance for acceptance, rather than trusting in the gift of God's grace through Yeshua's finished work on the tree.[35] Though this may or may not be full blown apostasy, it *is* cult-like behavior and shows a failure to understand the acceptance and fullness of spiritual life there is in Yeshua.

There may be many believing Gentiles who, though saved, still have personal growth, self-esteem or identity issues. They may think that conversion to traditional Judaism or Messianic Judaism will improve or fulfill who they are as a person. Such individuals should be getting pastoral counseling from the Word of God. It is *in Yeshua*, and His complete atonement, that we find our identity, life and purpose.

Therefore, *"Set your mind on the things above, not on the things that are on earth. For you have died and your life is hidden with Messiah in God."*[36]

YOUR PEOPLE, MY PEOPLE

Many times a Jewish believer and a Gentile believer will fall in love and desire to get married. There is more on 'Messianic Marriage' later in this book, but for now let me say this. When a Jewish believer marries a Gentile believer who doesn't understand Jewish culture, there can be tension and a tendency to find the Messianic life inconvenient and unworkable. I would advise counseling with your congregation leader. As in Ruth 1:16, *"Your people shall be my people, and your God, my God,"* the Gentile who marries the Jewish believer should be made aware that there are incumbent responsibilities of spiritual testimony, witness and calling in marrying into the Jewish people.

IN SUMMARY

In our unity we demonstrate the grace and love of God which being neither Jewish nor Gentile could produce in itself. Only in Yeshua is there full acceptance of those who are diverse in their cultural expression of the life of Yeshua. This is why we are exhorted to accept one another graciously as we have been graciously accepted by God in Messiah. *"Therefore, **accept one another**, just as Messiah also accepted us to the glory of God."*[37]

QUESTIONS
FOR YOUR FURTHER STUDY AND CONSIDERATION

How is the term 'Gentile' understood by the majority of Jewish people today? How can you counter the stereotypes that are so common?

Why is it important for both Jews and Gentiles to worship together in our congregations? What is the difference between unity and uniformity?

How can I as a Gentile believer express my faith in Messiah in order to be a light and witness to my Jewish friends?

FOOTNOTES

[1] *Mazel Tov*—'Congratulations' (Literally, 'Good Luck')
[2] see Ephesians 2:11,12
[3] see John 10:16
[4] Romans 11:13
[5] Romans 1:13; 11:25
[6] see Acts 22:3
[7] see Rev. 5:9
[8] see Acts 2
[9] Matthew 9:17
[10] Acts 10
[11] Acts 11:1-18
[12] see Acts 11:19-22
[13] Acts 15
[14] Acts 15:7-11
[15] see Galatians 2:11-15; 2 Cor. 11:22
[16] Romans 11:16-25
[17] Galatians 6:15
[18] see also John 4:21, 23, 24
[19] see Ephesians 3:1-6
[20] Ephesians 4:4
[21] Ephesians 4:3
[22] Ephesians 4:13
[23] see Mark 9:38-40
[24] Romans 15:7
[25] Ephesians 1:3
[26] Romans 4:11-13, 16
[27] see Colossians 2:10
[28] John 14:6; Col. 2:9,10; 1 John 1:7; 2:1
[29] 1 John 2:19
[30] Isaiah 44:6, John 8:58
[31] 1 Timothy 2:5
[32] John 14:6
[33] 1 John 2:22
[34] Ephesians 1:3
[35] see Philippians 3:1-9
[36] Colossians 3:2,3
[37] Romans 15:7; see also Romans 15:1-13

Chapter Three

Torah
and
The Messianic Believer

Then the LORD your God
will prosper you...
for the LORD will again
rejoice over you for good,
just as He rejoiced over your fathers;
if you obey the LORD your God
to keep His commandments
and His statutes which are written
in this book of the law,
if you turn to the LORD your God with
all your heart and soul.
— Moses
Deuteronomy 30:9,10

But we know that the Law is good,
if one uses it lawfully.
— Rabbi Shaul (Paul)
1 Timothy 1:8

Maybe it's because we're Messianic, or maybe it's just a question that's bound to be raised. In any case, the issue of the Torah (The Law, or the Mosaic Covenant) does seem to come up, especially as Jewish believers seek to live out their faith in Yeshua in a Jewish manner of lifestyle. After all, to some it would seem only natural that the way to demonstrate that Messianic faith is Jewish is by "keeping the Law."

In many cases this can lead to some confusion as to our relationship to the Torah. Some teach that believers in Messiah Yeshua, especially Jewish believers, are still under the Torah's authority for their fellowship, esteem and obedience. Others think that the Torah is totally irrelevant to the spiritual life and unworthy of serious study and application. What is the truth? We read in 2 Timothy 3:16,17…

> *All Scripture is inspired by God and profitable for teaching, for reproof, for correction, for training in righteousness; so that the man of God may be adequate, equipped for every good work.*

When Paul the Apostle (called *Rabbi Saul* or *Rav Shaul* by some) wrote that *"all Scripture is inspired by God and profitable"* we have to remember that the full body of New Covenant Scriptures was not yet written. As the apostolic writings became available, they were recognized *as Scripture* as well, as in 2 Peter 3:15,16. But at the time of Paul's writing he was primarily refering to the *Tanakh*—(*Torah* [Law], *Neviim* [Prophets] and *Kituvim* [Writings])—that is, the

Older Covenant. Regardless of modern ideas about the relevance or irrelevance of the Tanakh, the New Covenant writers considered it to be both *inspired* and *profitable*—useful to their work and growth as a people of God.

We also read in Romans 7:12 & 14, *"The Law is holy, and the commandment is holy and righteous and good...we know that the Law is spiritual..."* Therefore we are never to consider the Tanakh, (or the Torah as in this case) anything but *holy and righteous, good* and *spiritual* in our view of its teachings. We are to study the Tanakh thoroughly and learn its inspired truth, for if rightly understood, the Tanakh is spiritually *profitable* for our lives. Any congregation or church that is not doing so is leaving out two thirds of God's Word!

HOW DOES NEW COVENANT FAITH RELATE TO TORAH?

In Romans 3:28, Paul first demonstrates that a person is saved by faith through God's salvation in Messiah Yeshua, and not by any works of the Torah: *"For we maintain that a man is justified by faith apart from works of the Law."* Paul then seems to reinstate the relationship between faith and Law in verse 31 saying, *"Do we then make void the Law through faith? Certainly not! On the contrary, we establish the Law."* Amazingly, Paul writes that rather than making the Law void (or nullified) through our faith, it is actually established or confirmed by our faith in Messiah! In light of other Scriptures this raises two immediate questions:

1. How does our faith establish the Torah?
2. Doesn't Paul also teach that certain aspects of the Torah are nullified by New Covenant faith?

How does our faith establish Torah?

Paul wrote under the inspiration of Ruach HaKodesh (the Holy Spirit) in 2 Timothy 3:16,17 that *all Scripture*, (meaning the Older Covenant since the New Covenant was not yet fully written at that time), *is God inspired and profitable* for our adequacy as sons and servants of God.

✡ Mature faith sees that the Torah reveals the holiness and righteousness of God (Lev. 19:2; 1 Peter 1:15).
✡ Mature faith recognizes that the Torah reveals the fallen nature of man (Deut. 28:1,15; 1 Tim. 1:10).
✡ Mature faith recognizes that the Torah reveals as praiseworthy those who lived by faith in God, not by their own righteousness (Genesis 15:6, Hebrews 11).
✡ Mature faith discerns that the Torah witnesses to and leads one to Messiah (Gen. 49:10; Jeremiah 31:31; Galatians 4:19-25).

The Torah is still and will always be profitable. God forbid that anyone should reject any inspired text, especially that which our faith establishes!

But how exactly does our faith establish the Law? The Torah reveals our sins as "falling short" of God's standard, and therefore reveals us as condemned sinners. For Torah states that we *"are to be holy for the Lord our God is holy."*[1] By accepting Messiah's forgiveness and atonement we in effect acknowledge the rightness of the Law, and its judgment of us. For example, if a condemned criminal accepts a pardon, he is then admitting to the guilt of his crimes, and the law which rightly put him under condemnation. If he refuses to admit his guilt, he is therefore not entitled to receive the free gift of the pardon in good conscience. By faith in Yeshua we have accepted God's pardon and have thereby acknowledged our guilt and deserved condemnation,[2] and we are accepting and confirming the Torah's authority and validity to condemn us. Our faith therefore establishes the Law. If we were to deny the Law's authority to condemn, we would be denying the necessity of Yeshua's atonement to save and deliver us from our just condemnation under the Law.

KEEP THE TORAH...PERFECTLY?

Orthodox, or traditional Jews have a reputation for Law keeping and Torah-oriented worship. In actuality, they observe the *traditions of men*, rather than the *truth of God*, the Scriptures.[3] Orthodox Jews believe that keeping the traditions pleases God, even to the extent of forgiveness of sins and obtaining eternal life. For example, in the *Babylonian Talmud*, Shabbat 118b, it says, "Whoever is careful with Sabbath observance will be forgiven all his sins, even idolatry." In the rabbinical writing *Tanna DeBei Eliyahu* it says, "Whoever studies Torah Law every day is guaranteed to go to heaven."

Though rabbinical writings declare such things, it just isn't so. In fact, the Scriptures say otherwise, as is summed up in Deuteronomy 27:26—*"'Cursed is he who does not confirm the words of this law by doing them.' And all the people shall say, 'Amen.'"* The point is, NO ONE CAN PERFECTLY KEEP THE LAW. Therefore being under the condemnation of the Law, we are to be drawn to Messiah for mercy and forgiveness.[4]

By not seeing the Scriptures for what they actually say, these same sincere people do not view themselves as hopeless and condemned sinners as the Torah declares we all are. Thus they do not see the need for a Savior, particularly Messiah Yeshua. Tragically they reject the only means of forgiveness God has provided. In so doing, despite their supposed devotion to the Torah, rather than establishing the Torah, their unbelief denies the very purpose of the Torah they are reputed to observe. We need to pray for our people who are supposedly following the Law, but in fact contradict it by not believing in Messiah Yeshua, God's only way of salvation. To *say* we believe the Scriptures is one thing. But Yeshua very plainly said, *"For if you believed Moses, you would believe Me; for he wrote of Me. But if you do not believe his writings, how will you believe My words?"*[5] Let me reiterate: if Orthodox Jews, or anyone for that matter, actually observed the Torah, they would realize their need for the atonement that only Messiah Yeshua has provided.

ARE CERTAIN ASPECTS OF THE TORAH NULLIFIED IN THE NEW COVENANT?

The Greek word that Paul uses in Romans 3:31 for "make void" or "nullify" is *katargeo*. The basic sense of this word is *"to cause to be idle or useless."* The term always denotes a superior power coming in to supercede the power previously in effect—just as light nullifies or replaces darkness.

TORAH'S AUTHORITY IS NULLIFIED

In Romans 7, Paul uses this same Greek word *katargeo* to describe how the authority of the marriage relationship is ended upon the death of a spouse: *"For the married woman is bound by law to her husband while he is living; but if her husband dies, she is released from the law concerning the husband."*[6] Here *katargeo* is translated *released*. Paul is showing that we were essentially "married" to the Law, and therefore under its jurisdiction and authority.[7] He goes on to say that in Messiah we died to the Law that we might be joined, or spiritually married as it were, to Yeshua.[8] Thus we are released from the Law's authority, and are under the new jurisdiction and authority of our new Husband, Messiah! *"But now we have been released from the Law, having died to that by which we were bound, so that we serve in newness of the Spirit and not in oldness of the letter."*[9] The Law no longer has jurisdiction over our lives. We have liberty through our trust in and submission to Messiah.

From this portion we see that faith in Messiah

does not nullify the Law's *purpose*, but that the Law's *authority* over New Covenant believers has in fact been nullified, just as prison no longer has authority over those pardoned. We therefore can develop our first principle from this truth for those of mature faith:

1. *Mature faith does not submit to the Law, but enjoys the liberty of faith in Messiah Yeshua.*

This does not mean that we are "lawless", but we are under the authority of the Messianic "Torah" of our new Husband, Messiah, and His New Covenant with us.[10]

TORAH'S GLORY IS NULLIFIED

In 2 Corinthians 3:4-14, we see Paul's *midrash* (comments and teaching) on Exodus 34:29-35, where he again uses the word *katargeo*.[11] In this section Paul is saying that the Law came with a certain glory, or splendor; but he teaches that the glory that came by the Torah had certain limitations.

> *But if the ministry of death in letters engraved on stones, came with glory, so that the sons of Israel could not look intently at the face of Moses because of the glory of his face, fading as it was, how will the ministry of the Spirit fail to be even more with glory* (v.7,8).

The stones Paul refers to are the two stone tablets on which were written the Ten Commandments. Here Paul states that the glory Moses received in the Law—*"in letters engraved on stones"*— was *"fading away"* (*katargeo*). The New Covenant glory exceeds and surpasses the fading glory of the Law.

Condemnation, the very result of our trangression of the Law, was demonstrated in the limited glory that could be derived by the Law.

> *For if the ministry of condemnation has glory, much more does the ministry of righteousness abound in glory. For indeed what had glory, in this case has no glory because of the glory that surpasses it. For if that which fades away was with glory, much more that which remains is in glory* (2 Cor. 3:9-11).

The Holy Spirit through the New Covenant gives a glory far surpassing the glory of the Law. The Torah's glory was to "*fade away*"—that is, be nullified—but the New Covenant's glory is to *remain,* and is in fact, eternal. Thus, in light of the surpassing glory and honor that we have in the New Covenant, we are to be bold in our ministry, not like Moses who had to hide his fading glory, but we proclaim the truth openly "without veils."

> *Therefore having such a hope, we use great boldness in our speech, and are not like Moses, who used to put a veil over his face so that the sons of Israel would not look intently at the end of what was fading away*
> (2 Cor. 3:12,13).

At first Moses wore the veil so as to not blind those around him from God's glory.[12] After a period of time the purpose of the veil was to hide the fact that the glory Moses received when he received the Torah was *fading away*—a glory that began to fade as soon as he left the Lord's presence.

> *But their minds were hardened; for until this very day at the reading of the old covenant the same veil remains unlifted, because it is removed in Messiah*
> (2 Cor. 3:14).

As that veil prevented our ancestors from seeing the fading glory, so also the *hardness*—a spiritual insensitivity—is like a veil over many of our people's minds today. At the reading of Torah most still do not see that Messiah is the end, or the goal of the Law.[13] I say many of our people's minds, but not all—this hardness upon Israel is *in part*,[14] even as a hardness is upon the Gentiles.[15] In fact, just as Moses *removed the veil* when he stood before the Lord,[16] 'the veil of hardness' is actually *removed* (*katargeo*) by faith in Messiah Yeshua—the same Lord before Whom Moses stood. In Messiah, the veil or *hardness* over our minds is removed by grace, and replaced with the greater and lasting glory of the New Covenant.

Please note that the one replaces the other. You cannot have both the glory of the Torah *and* the glory of the Spirit. People who are trying to gain honor, glory or self-esteem through obedience to Torah are not enjoying the greater glory of liberty, honor and confidence in Messiah. They soon find that the Law's fading glory only reveals where they *"fall short of the glory of God."*[17]

If we look to Yeshua and receive the cleansing, acceptance in the Beloved, and His assurance of eternal salvation we can live openly, transparently, honestly—"without veils." We receive this grace in which we stand through the Holy Spirit in view of the finished work of Messiah upon the cross, for He is *"the Lord our righteousness."*[18] In Messiah we have the certainty of His glory, even as we have the liberty in regards to the Law's authority. We therefore can develop a second principle from this section:

> 2. *Mature faith does not glory in the Law of Moses, but has confidence in Messiah's New Covenant.* Our "boast" is in Yeshua alone.[19]

TORAH'S HOSTILITY IS NULLIFIED

As we think of what our faith has provided in Messiah and His New Covenant, we cannot overlook the final application of the word *katargeo* in Ephesians 2:14-16.

> *For He [Messiah] Himself is our peace, who made both groups into one and broke down the barrier of the dividing wall, by abolishing in His flesh the enmity, which is the Law of commandments contained in ordinances, so that in Himself He might make the two into one new man, thus establishing peace, and might reconcile them both in one body to God through the cross, by it having put to death the enmity.*

Outside the Temple courts in Jerusalem was a partition, or dividing wall called the *Soreg*, which symbolized the enmity or hostility between Jews and heathen Gentiles. Beyond this barrier heathens were not permitted to approach the Temple area. In fact, the *Soreg* contained an inscription forbidding a Gentile from going any farther upon pain of death.[20] In Acts 21:28, an uproar occurred when Paul was accused of taking Trophimus beyond the *Soreg*.

The enmity symbolized in the *Soreg* existed to maintain the purity of God's worship and testimony from any defiling pagan elements. The Law directed Israel to live in such a way that they would be separate in lifestyle and beliefs from the nations, and to have enmity toward the sinful practices of their paganism.[21] Once Yeshua had died for and cleansed sins, the cause of the enmity was no longer there—it was *abolished* [*katargeo*] *in His flesh*. Thus the *Soreg* was no longer needed; for Jew and Gentile believers are made one family in Messiah!

From this section we see that the enmity produced by the Law is nullified in regards to believers. We therefore can establish our third principle:

3. *Mature faith does not segregate or exclude other believers on the basis of the Law, but we have unity with all believers in Messiah.*

There are no second class believers in Yeshua. If we have been accepted by grace, we are to accept one another graciously as well.

THREE PRINCIPLES OF MATURE FAITH

To summarize, from these sections we see that though faith may not nullify the Law, the Law's *authority*, *glory* and *enmity* over believers are in fact nullified. We see three principles from these truths for people of mature faith:

1. AUTHORITY: *Mature faith does not submit to the Law's authority, but enjoys the liberty in our submission to Messiah.* Not that we are "lawless," but we are under the authority of the Messianic "Torah" of our new Husband's Brit

Chadasha (New Covenant).[22] In this regard, we are further taught in Colossians 2:16,17— *"Therefore no one is to act as your judge in regard to food or drink or in respect to a festival or a new moon or a Sabbath day—things which are a mere shadow of what is to come; but the substance belongs to Messiah."* You may enjoy the festival or not, the food laws or not, and no one is to judge you one way or another. Why? For all these issues are a *foreshadowing* of Messiah: they picture Him! Therefore, as these *things* point to Yeshua our Messiah, they are a meaningful testimony of Him.

2. GLORY: *Mature faith does not glory in the Law, but has confidence in Messiah.* Our boast is in Him alone: *"'Let him who boasts [glories] boast of this,* **that he understands and knows Me**, *that I am the LORD who exercises loving-kindness, justice, and righteousness on earth; for I delight in these things,' declares the LORD."*[23]

3. ENMITY: *Mature faith does not segregate by the Law, but has unity with all believers in Messiah.* We therefore accept one another as Yeshua has accepted each of us.[24]

IN MESSIAH: THE FULFILLMENT OF THE TORAH

Romans 3:31 does not teach that we are still under the Mosaic Torah, but rather by faith in Messiah we are freed from the Law, recognizing its authority and thereby establishing it. In the same way, Messiah's teaching in Matthew 5:17-20 is to be understood:

"Do not think that I came to abolish the Law or the Prophets; I did not come to abolish but to fulfill. 18 For truly I say to you, until heaven and earth pass away, not the smallest letter or stroke shall pass from the Law until all is accomplished. 19 Whoever then annuls one of the least of these commandments, and teaches others to do the same, shall be called least in the kingdom of heaven; but whoever keeps and teaches them, he shall be called great in the kingdom of heaven. 20 "For I say to you that unless your righteousness surpasses that of the scribes and Pharisees, you will not enter the kingdom of heaven" (Matthew 5:17-20).

Messiah does not destroy but fulfills the Mosaic Torah (Law). In so doing Yeshua provides us with the righteousness to which all the Torah pointed (Rom 10:4). His fulfillment of the Mosaic Torah does not bring an end to it—exactly the opposite! Our faith does not nullify the Law, but establishes it by recognizing its authority to condemn. Thus revealing our need for pardon, forgiveness, and mercy. Also, Messiah's fulfillment of the Torah actually establishes the Torah as the standard for righteousness that He alone can provide. (Rom. 3:31; Gal. 2:21) By His singular fulfillment He now grants to all who believe on Him that very righteousness that the Mosaic Torah demands.

Therefore, anyone attempting to "lower the bar" of righteousness by annulling even the least of the commandments as Matthew 5:19 states, not only removes the standard that brings us to recognize our need for mercy but, also intimates that Yeshua's death was unnecessary for our sin.

My greatness in heaven is determined by forever knowing Yeshua as the fulfiller not the nullifier of all the Torah. My righteousness can only surpass the Pharisees by my trusting in the One who fulfilled it all and deposited it to my account by faith (2 Cor 5:21).

Thus, mature faith not only establishes the Law by trusting in Yeshua for salvation, but also enjoys the liberty, certainty, and unity provided graciously in Messiah Yeshua!

HOW THEN SHOULD WE INTEREPT THE TORAH?

The question now arises, "How do we as Messianic believers interpret and apply the teachings of the Tanakh in general, and the Torah in particular?" This question was raised by first century Messianic believers as well, and the answer then is the same answer for today. Paul wrote to Timothy about this very matter:

> *But we know that the Torah is good, if one uses it lawfully, realizing the fact that Torah is not made for a righteous person, but for those who are lawless and rebellious, for the ungodly and sinners, for the unholy and profane, for those who kill their fathers or mothers, for murderers and immoral men and homosexuals and kidnappers and liars and perjurers, and whatever else is contrary to sound teaching, according to the glorious gospel of the blessed God, with which I have been entrusted* (1 Timothy 1:8-11).

In this portion Paul, a Jewish believer, is speaking to Timothy, another Jewish believer, about Torah. In Ephesus where Timothy was ministering for Messiah, there were false teachers that were teaching strange doctrines because of their misunderstanding of the Torah. Paul informed Timothy that false teachers misunderstood the purpose of the Torah, and therefore misapplied it. These false teachers focused attention on Torah, rather than Messiah. This led to them straying from the truth and eventually shipwrecking their faith![25] Such teaching was wrong then, and is still wrong today. Paul explains that Torah's purpose as Law is not for the righteous, but for the wicked. In this portion when Paul uses the term 'righteous', he means those whom God has declared righteous *in Messiah*.[26] False teachers did not, and *still* do not understand the Torah's purpose—to reveal to us our spiritual need for forgiveness found *only* in Yeshua.[27] Paul clarifies this by reiterating to Timothy nine of the Ten Commandments.[28]

- ✡ 1st *Thou shalt have no other gods before me—* **lawless and rebellious...**
- ✡ 2nd *Thou shalt not make unto thee any graven image...for I the LORD thy God am a jealous God, punishing the iniquity...of them that hate Me—***ungodly and sinners...**
- ✡ 3rd *Thou shalt not take the name of the LORD thy God in vain—***unholy and profane...**
- ✡ 5th *Honour thy father and thy mother—***kill their fathers or mothers...**
- ✡ 6th *Thou shalt not kill—***murderers...**
- ✡ 7th *Thou shalt not commit adultery—***immoral men and homosexuals...**
- ✡ 8th *Thou shalt not steal—***kidnappers** (literally *men stealers*)...
- ✡ 9th *Thou shalt not bear false witness against thy neighbor—***liars and perjurers...**

✣ 10ᵗʰ*Thou shalt not covet thy neighbor's house...thy neighbor's wife, etc.*—covetousness is noted as anything else ***that is contrary to sound teaching***.

PUT ON YOUR 'GOSPEL GLASSES'

Paul then states that this *sound teaching* is understood *according to the glorious gospel.* How do you recognize *sound teaching*? Notice the word *according*. The standard for sound teaching is when it is *according to* the Good News of Messiah, the *"glorious gospel of the blessed God."* For example, I need my glasses to see with, obviously. Without them I can see a page, but I can't read what is written on it, nor know what it really says. Just as glasses bring into focus what is written on the page, the Gospel brings into focus the purpose of the Torah. These false teachers did not submit their teaching regarding Torah to the Gospel, therefore they misinterpreted the Torah. The New Covenant enables us to rightly understand, and to apply the Torah. Without the Good News, Torah shows us our sins, to then lead us to Messiah, Who is the goal of the Torah.[29] But in Messiah, and through the 'Gospel glasses', Torah is now "profitable" and edifying for your soul.[30] This is why Paul consistently states *that for the believer* Torah was written for our encouragement.[31]

HEY, WHAT HAPPENED TO THE SABBATH?

Did you notice that in Paul's listing of the Ten Commandments, Paul omits the fourth commandment—*Remember the Sabbath day*?

This is the one commandment *not repeated* in the New Covenant, because the deeper issue of Shabbat rest is revealed—the rest which is found only in Messiah Himself.[32] Messianic believers meet on Shabbat, not out of obligation, but to enjoy our liberty in the Lord, and to glorify Him.[33]*

So, study the Scriptures, knowing as Yeshua said, it's all about Him.[34] The entire Word of God[35] is His spiritual nourishment for you, to be enjoyed and employed. May He who inspired the Scriptures illuminate your mind to its truth, and empower you to live out that very truth—all to the glory of Yeshua our Messiah!

QUESTIONS
FOR YOUR FURTHER STUDY AND CONSIDERATION

How is the Law's authority nullified in Messiah? Please explain.

Explain how the enmity between Jew and non-Jew is nullified in Messiah, and how you can demonstrate this in your own life.

As a New Covenant believer, how does your faith *establish* Torah?

Name the three principles of 'Mature Faith'.

How does the New Covenant help us interpret and apply the Torah?

FOOTNOTES

[1] Leviticus 19:2, 1 Peter 1:16
[2] Daniel 12:2; Matthew 25:26
[3] see Matthew 15:1-13
[4] see Galatians 3:24
[5] John 5:46, 47
[6] Romans 7:2
[7] Romans 7:1
[8] Romans 7:4
[9] Romans 7:6
[10] Luke 22:20; 1 Cor. 9:20, 21
[11] 2 Cor. 3:7,11,13,14
[12] Exodus 34:29-35
[13] see Romans 10:4
[14] see Romans 11:25
[15] see Ephesians 4:18
[16] Ex. 34:34
[17] Romans 3:23
[18] Jer. 23:5,6; 1 John 2:1
[19] see 1 Cor. 1:30, 31
[20] Midd.2:3; Yoma 16a; Josephus, Antiq. VIII. 3,2; Wars, v. 5,2
[21] see Lev. 26:30; Isa.44:10-18
[22] Jer. 31:31-34, Mt. 11:28,29; 1 Cor. 9:20,21
[23] Jer.9:24,25, 1 Cor.1:30, 31
[24] Romans 15:7
[25] 1 Timothy 1:19,20
[26] see 2 Cor. 5:21
[27] see Galatians 3:23-25
[28] see Exodus 20
[29] Romans 10:4
[30] 2 Tim. 3:16
[31] see Rom. 15:4; 1 Cor. 10:11
[32] see Mt. 11:28; Heb. 4:1-11
[33] see Colossians 2:16-21
[34] John 5:39; Rom. 10:4; Heb.10:1
[35] Acts 20:27

*For further study on keeping Shabbat, see WMM's book *The Feasts of Israel.*

Chapter Four

Considering Synagogues, Churches, Messianic Congregations

I WAS GLAD WHEN THEY SAID TO ME,
"LET US GO TO THE HOUSE OF THE LORD"
— DAVID
PSALM 122:1

HE WHO WALKS WITH WISE MEN
WILL BE WISE — SOLOMON
PROVERBS 13:20A

The story is told of the Jewish man who was stranded on a desert island. When his rescuers arrived they noticed that there were three huts that the man had built. They asked about them and he responded, "Well the first hut there, that's where I live.

The second hut, that's my synagogue that I attend every Shabbat." "What about that third hut? What's it for?", his rescuers asked. The man replied brusquely, "That's a synagogue that I wouldn't set foot in!"

Finding a place to worship and fellowship is important, and it can be difficult to find a place where we fit in and are accepted for who we are. People often ask, "Where should Messianic believers go to worship?" The issue is too often answered pragmatically, "Whatever is closest." Others think that a Messianic believer should never go to a Gentile cultured church, but only go to a Messianic congregation. And still others may say, "Who needs fellowship at all?" What is the correct answer? Let's consider this issue carefully.

Should Messianic Believers Attend a Traditional Synagogue?

At the risk of sounding double-minded, the answer is both yes and no. When invited to a Bar Mitzvah, marriage ceremony, funeral or other special events there is no problem celebrating the joy, or sharing the grief with the individuals involved.

That being said, the traditional synagogue is *not* a sufficient worship experience to satisfy what our souls need, and what God expects. For the purpose of spiritual worship, a place where Yeshua's name is despised is not the place for believers to be found for worship and fellowship.

Though the teaching may be historically, culturally or socially helpful; and though the congregants friendly; and though the atmosphere may feel familiar; still, our worship must be *in Spirit* and *in truth*,[1] and must exalt that Name which is above every name—Yeshua. Where He is not welcomed, I do not want to be accepted.

We read of this issue in Scripture:
> *For the bodies of those animals whose blood is brought into the holy place by the high priest as an offering for sin, are burned outside the camp. Therefore Yeshua also, that He might sanctify the people through His own blood, suffered outside the gate. So, let us go out to Him outside the camp, bearing His reproach. While He is rejected and outside the camp, so we too bear His reproach as we follow Him* (Hebrews 13:11-13).

This does not mean that we are to have a martyr complex about the matter. In all ways we are to be loving and friendly to all our people, though we painfully recognize that part of the cost of identifying with Messiah is also identifying with His rejection.[2]

SHOULD MESSIANIC BELIEVERS WORSHIP IN GENTILE CHURCHES?

Believers, Jewish or Gentile, should love all other believers, and should never look down on one another because of cultural, racial, societal, or national differences.

That being said, there are some congregations that are more helpful to furthering Messianic growth and testimony than others. Frankly, today most churches are clueless of the need for Jewish believers to maintain their identity and help their Jewish children to grow as Jewish believers as well. Therefore most churches do not have a discipleship program to help Messianic believers grow as Jewish believers. These churches may end up not so much discipling a Jewish believer in the Lord, but merely acculturating the new believer to the Gentile church culture and practice. Even worse, some churches actually teach that Jewish believers are *not Jewish* anymore! Beyond this, the normative Jewish *and* biblical culture which is ordered around the yearly festivals is generally overlooked as nothing more than a "custom of the Jews." Often the Jewish believers end up losing the natural biblical touchstones of our people, and the very roots of the Messianic, and biblical faith.

The Jewish children in such a church atmosphere end up with a non-Jewish frame of reference for their faith, and for all practical purposes, end up as non-Jews in their faith perspective. True, there are some Jewish believers who can *and do* survive as Messianic Jewish believers in a church setting, and don't consider themselves *former* Jews. These are exceptional—and the exception proves the rule—because sadly, most do not.

SHOULD A MESSIANIC BELIEVER ONLY ATTEND A MESSIANIC CONGREGATION?

This depends once more on several issues. Just because a fellowship is called a "Messianic congregation" doesn't mean it's a biblically based congregation in the true sense of the term. A congregation—and a church as well—must be properly organized in order to be a worship center, instruction center, fellowship center, and an evangelistic/outreach center. A congregation must be more than a weekly Bible study, or a monthly fellowship meeting. A congregation needs to be a place where disciples are in genuine, loving accountability to one another in the Lord.

Beyond this, a congregation needs to be a wholesome, loving place—not merely a 'non-Gentile' place that engenders anti-Gentile attitudes. Messianic does *not* and should not equate to anti-Gentile. If the choice is between an unwholesome, chauvinistic, unbiblically based 'Messianic congregation,' and a wholesome, loving, and biblically sound church, there really is no choice: go with the church, but know that as a Messianic believer you will have to personally maintain your messianic identity at home, and in rearing your children.

Of course, there is generally not this kind of extreme distinction, but I want to make the point clear: a biblically wholesome Gentile-cultured church is better than a non-biblically oriented Messianic congregation.

To Be or Not To Be ...Jewish?

The real question is this: "Will a Jewish believer live as a Jew, or not?" Let's look at the book of Esther to understand the importance of this issue for you and your children.

Purim is a biblical holiday taken from the Book of Esther. By the end of the book, Esther and her uncle Mordecai are the heroes of this historical account, but earlier in the story they had some weak moments.

> *Esther did not make known her people or her kindred, for Mordecai had instructed her that she should not make them known.*
> *Esther had not yet made known her kindred or her people, even as Mordecai had commanded her; for Esther did what Mordecai told her as she had done when under his care* (Esther 2:10,20).

For whatever reason, Esther wouldn't identify with our people. How could such a situation come up? Would not the king want to know the background of his potential wife? Was there a "don't ask, don't tell" policy in the Persian harem? No, without a doubt Esther would have been asked about her background before becoming queen, but she didn't tell. Presumably, she lied about it.

Why didn't Esther reveal she was a Jew? Perhaps the question for many then—and now—is, "What good does it do to tell people I'm a Jew?" Was Mordecai waiting for an auspicious time in order to save the Jewish people? This would be illogical since anti-Semitism didn't rear its head till several years later. In fact, if the Queen was known openly as a Jew, the case may be made that this might have made Haman think twice before staring a pogrom against the Queen's people. Was Mordecai just concerned that Esther might not attain to the queenly position if she revealed her Jewishness *before* her appointment as Queen? No, since she did not reveal it afterwards either.[3] Rather, Mordecai's advice seems to have been given out of concern for Esther's safety.[4] Perhaps then as now, there were many who feared they may lose something by identifying themselves as Jews, or as believers. But it was bad advice that almost backfired on him.[5]

Don't Ask, Don't Tell?

This "don't tell" policy has always been a problem for God's people. It leads to a bad testimony, and by some is seen as mere cowardice. As great a man as Abraham was, in order to save his own skin he didn't tell King Abimelech that Sarah was his wife, but instead said that she was his sister![6] In fact, Abraham committed this deceit twice.[7] This same problem also apparently influenced his son Isaac.[8]

This might be seen as a "better safe than sorry" plan by some, but in God's eyes not telling the truth is just plain sin. The Scriptures say:

> *Now if a person sins after he hears a public adjuration to testify when he is a witness, whether he has seen or otherwise known, if he does not tell it, then he will bear his guilt* (Leviticus 5:1).

Esther may not have been the only one not identifying as a Jew. Through the prophets, God had called back His people to the land of Israel. Those who heeded God's call left Babylon, but for some, life was pretty good in Babylon so they chose to stay there. In so doing, the Jewish people of Babylon did not identify with the call of God, and therefore did not identify themselves as the people of God. It is the same principle for us. If you will not identify with God's call you will not identify with God's people. After all, as soon as it was mentioned they were Jews it would be said, "But I thought the Jews were called back to Israel by God? Why are you still here?" Their unbelief and resulting shame would be revealed.

THE GODLY IDENTIFY WITH THE JEWISH PEOPLE

Principle: those who identify with God's purpose identify with God's people. Identifying with the call of God has always been evidenced by identifying with the people of God. Notice this in the life of Moses.

> *By faith Moses, when he had grown up, refused to be called the son of Pharaoh's daughter, choosing rather to endure ill-treatment with the people of God than to enjoy the passing pleasures of sin, considering the reproach of Messiah greater riches than the treasures of Egypt; for he was looking to the reward* (Hebrews 11:24-26).

Though it meant Daniel had to break the law rather than break faith with God, he still identified with his people and his homeland.

> *Now when Daniel knew that the document was signed, he entered his house (now in his roof chamber he had windows open toward Jerusalem); and he continued kneeling on his knees three times a day, praying and giving thanks before his God, as he had been doing previously* (Daniel 6:10).

Though not Jewish herself, Ruth pro-actively identified with the Jewish people when she identified with the God of Israel.

> *But Ruth said, "Do not urge me to leave you or turn back from following you; for where you go, I will go, and where you lodge, I will lodge. Your people shall be my people, and your God, my God"* (Ruth 1:16).

Though Paul was called to the Gentiles he recognized himself as a Jew and identified himself with his people throughout his ministry.

> *But Paul said, "I am a Jew of Tarsus in Cilicia...I am a Jew, born in Tarsus of Cilicia"* (Acts 21:39; 22:3).
> *I say then, God has not rejected His people has He? May it never be! For I too am an Israelite, a descendant of Abraham, of the tribe of Benjamin. God will not forsake a people who He foreknew!* (Romans 11:1,2).

Why did Paul do this? Was it mere ethnic chauvinism? No. By identifying with *God's people* Paul was identifying with *God's promises*, and unchanging purpose.

This may have been Paul's commitment, but what was his influence on other Jewish believers? Ask Timothy!

> *Paul came also to Derbe and to Lystra. And a disciple was there, named Timothy, the son of a Jewish woman who was a believer, but his father was a Greek, and he was well spoken of by the brethren who were in Lystra and Iconium. Paul wanted this man to go with him; and he took him and circumcised him because of the Jews who were in those parts, for they all knew that his father was a Greek* (Acts 16:1-3).

Paul identifies Timothy as a Jew through circumcision. Why? Who would know?

Timothy would know—and the *"Jews in those parts"* would know with certainty that faith in Yeshua was not a denial of the promises made to Israel, but the fulfillment of those promises! Whether it was Daniel, Joseph, Moses, Paul or Timothy (or you), the challenge of faith is always, "Do we believe God will be faithful to His promises?" If we do, will we identify with Him and His people?

No Middle Ground

Failure to identify with God's purpose and people is an age-old issue. By staying in Babylon the Jewish people weren't recognizable as *God's people*. God loves and cares for His people, therefore He confronted the problem head-on by allowing a Haman to arise and force the issue.[9]

Gentile believers need to identify with the Jewish people as well. They can do this by standing against anti-Semitism, proactively sharing Good News with Jewish people, praying for the Peace of Jerusalem, and identifying with the remnant of Israel— the Jewish believers in Yeshua. That's why so many Bible believing Gentiles attend Messianic congregations: they are identifying with God's unfailing promise to Israel by identifying with God's people.[10]

Am Yisrael Chai!

Jewish believers need to identify themselves and their children as Jews. When we as Jewish believers raise our children in a Gentile church culture, our kids might think we are subtly saying to them, "Don't tell them you're a Jew."

This is one reason Messianic congregations are available—to help Jewish believers to grow spiritually, and to testify powerfully *"Am Yisrael Chai B'Yeshua HaMashiach" – "the People of Israel Live in Yeshua the Messiah!"* Even so, Jewish believers quite often wander from church to church, and eventually are assimilated in a Gentile culture rather than identifying with their people. Why do they avoid messianic fellowship? There may be many understandable reasons, but by not identifying with the Jewish people, they're not *clearly* identifying with the call and purpose of God for the Jews.

YESHUA: A JEW'S JEW

Ben Elohim, the Son of God, came in the flesh, identifying Himself with all people.[11] He took on human form in order to die for the sins of all humanity. Not only this, Messiah could have come as a some mighty Babylonian, Persian or Roman Emperor, but chose rather to be identified as a Jew, even as a humble Jewish carpenter. How different Messiah was than Esther. Messiah identified with His Jewish people in His incarnation:

> *He came to His own, and those who were His own did not receive Him* (John 1:11);
> *For I say that Messiah has become a servant to the circumcision on behalf of the truth of God to confirm the promises given to the fathers* (Romans 15:8);
> *He is not ashamed to call them brethren* (Heb. 2:11).

If Messiah had come as a Roman, that might have gained Him more privileges, or by coming as a Greek, more respect.

But Messiah came as a Jew to identify with the purposes, prophecies and promises of God.[12] God chose us, the Jewish people, not because we're the brightest or greatest, or most spiritual, but because we're the least of all peoples.[13] He chose us in order to demonstrate to the whole world that His grace, not our greatness, is enough to keep us. Yeshua therefore came in utter weakness as a Jew, as *"a root out of dry gound,"*[14] to demonstrate the sufficiency of God's eternal grace. Like Paul in Romans 11:1,2, every Jewish believer testifies that God's gracious promise fulfilled in Messiah is still sufficient for all who will believe.

Yeshua identified with the call and purpose of God, therefore He identified with us, because He loves us. If we're ashamed of identifying with the Jewish people are we not denying the purpose of God in Messiah? This is why Paul proclaims his Jewish identity in the book of Romans—not to boast in 'the flesh,' but to boast in a God Whose promises are true, and Who will not forsake Israel.

THE MOST JEWISH THING YOU CAN DO

Have you come to faith in Messiah yet? Messiah is willing to identify with you—He died for your sins. Will you identify with Him and receive His salvation? As meaningful as the land of Israel is, Messiah Yeshua is the true eternal refuge and security for our people, *and all people.* To *not* come to Him is equivalent to staying in Babylon, as with Esther's generation. God is calling us to faith in Messiah. Must it take another Haman to awake us from our spiritual lethargy?

Just as it was disobedience to stay in Babylon after God fulfilled His promises to free them, it's also disobedience not to come to Yeshua after God has fulfilled His promises to bring Messiah.

Esther repented[15] and became a hero. If you repent, you too can play a significant role in God's work in this world. Those who identify with God's purpose identify with God's people. If you are a believer and have a Jewish background, isn't it time you identify with *your* people? If you're a Gentile believer, will you identify with Israel and commit to pray for the peace of Jerusalem? Messiah identified with us to save us; those who identify with Him will love those whom He loves.

So if you're a Jewish believer, find a congregation that will help you grow spiritually strong, and have a proper balance on the issues of your Jewish identity and biblical faith. Yes, finding a congregation can be a trying experience. In the next chapter you will find some guidelines on selecting a congregation which will help take some of the guesswork and stress out of the decision-making process. Be assured that God will lead you through this adventure, as you take what is an all-important step of obedience in following the Lord.

QUESTIONS
FOR YOUR FURTHER STUDY AND CONSIDERATION

What do you consider important when selecting a place for you and your family to worship? Why?

Why, at times, have Jewish people hidden their Jewish identity throughout history? Is this a problem today?

As a believer in Messiah, where has God led you for fellowship? Why do you believe this?

FOOTNOTES
[1] see John 4:23,24
[2] see Is. 53:3; 1 Peter 4:12-16
[3] Esther 2:20
[4] Esther 2:11
[5] Esther 4:12
[6] See Genesis 12: 11-18
[7] see Genesis 20:2-11
[8] Genesis 26:7-10
[9] see Esther 3
[10] Jeremiah 31:35-37; Romans 11:1-6
[11] Philippians 2:5-8
[12] see Genesis 12:3, 49:10, Deuteronomy 18:15, Micah 5:2
[13] see Deut. 7:6-8; 9:6
[14] Isaiah 53:2
[15] Esther 4:16

Chapter Five

FINDING A GOOD CONGREGATION

> LET US CONSIDER
> HOW TO STIMULATE ONE ANOTHER
> TO LOVE AND GOOD DEEDS,
> NOT FORSAKING
> OUR OWN ASSEMBLING TOGETHER...
> HEBREWS 10:24,25A

> MY SOUL LONGED AND EVEN YEARNED
> FOR THE COURTS OF THE LORD;
> MY HEART AND MY FLESH
> SING FOR JOY
> TO THE LIVING GOD.
> — DAVID
> PSALM 84:2

The biblical instruction for fellowship is that believers, all believers, should be in regular weekly fellowship with others of like faith.

> *Let us hold fast the confession of our hope without wavering, for He who promised is faithful; and let us consider how to stimulate one another to love and good deeds, not forsaking our own assembling together, as is the habit of some, but encouraging one another; and all the more as you see the day drawing near* (Hebrews 10:23-25).

The question then arises, "Where should I go for fellowship?" There are five simple principles that have helped me, and that can help you to find a place of worship for you and your family. Of course, these principles assume that you and your family are praying for the Lord's guidance on the matter, and that you are actively seeking fellowship.

1) DOES THE CONGREGATION'S DOCTRINAL STATEMENT AGREE WITH WHAT YOU BELIEVE ABOUT GOD AND THE BIBLE?

This is vital, for Amos 3:3 states, *"Can two walk together, unless they are agreed?"* In other words, you can't walk with another unless you have agreed on where it is you are going. If you're walking north, and your friend is walking south, you both are walking, but certainly not together. Similarly, you need to agree with the basic teachings of the congregation that you want to associate with. Don't *assume* that you do.

The congregation should have a 'statement of faith'—a list, or description of what they believe about the Scriptures. If the congregation does not, this can mean that it is uncertain what it believes as a fellowship. This will not provide you much stability as you seek to spiritually grow in the Lord.

Of course, this assumes that *you know* what you believe. It would be good to write down the 5-10 basic truths you are convinced of regarding your faith. This should include what you believe about:
- ✡ Messiah's nature and atonement
- ✡ The Holy Spirit's nature and activity
- ✡ The Scripture's authority in matters of faith and practice, etc.

In the appendix of this book is a statement of faith that might be helpful to you as you consider this vital issue.

2) ARE THE GOALS OF THE CONGREGATION IN LINE WITH GOD'S CALL UPON YOUR LIFE?

If you are desirous of helping to reach the world with the Good News, and the congregation doesn't have a burden for the world, then we're talking major disagreement here. And yes, a congregation—even Messianic congregations—should be burdened to reach the *entire* world with the Good News of Messiah!

If you have children, it is God's call for you to raise these children in the truth of God's word. Does the congregation have a good children's program, or at least is it firmly committed to having a good one? It should be.

How do you find this out? By asking questions as you visit with the congregation leader, at the membership class, at membership follow-up interviews, or simply by carefully observing what's going on.

3) DOES THE CONGREGATION HAVE OPPORTUNITY FOR YOU TO GROW AND SERVE IN LIGHT OF YOUR GIFTING IN THE LORD?

The congregation is a place for you to grow spiritually. It should serve as a worship center, a 'witness center', and a 'word center.' To grow spiritually, not only are you to be taught the Word of God from both the pulpit and through personal discipleship, but you are also to be given the opportunity to serve the Lord. The assembly of believers is called the "body of Messiah"[1] for a reason. God has gifted every believer, and the congregation is to provide opportunity for each believer's serving and speaking gifts to develop. This allows believers to minister to others within the fellowship, and through outreach to the world at large.

4) DOES THE CONGREGATION VALUE PROPER STEWARDSHIP OF ITS RESOURCES?

There are three areas, or commodities that a congregation must handle well. They are *finances, time,* and *people*.

MONEY MATTERS

Is the only person who knows about the congregation's money the congregation leader? This is questionable. Legally and ethically there should be a board of trustees that handles the finances of the congregation. In fact, the congregation leader should have very little actual control over the finances. His job is that of spiritual leadership. The budget should be established in line with the spiritual priorities of the congregation as set yearly by the *Zakanim* (Elders) and approved by the congregation at an annual business meeting. But the actual handling of the finances of the congregation should be done so that there is no hint of impropriety, nor opportunity for rumors regarding the leadership's stewardship of the congregation's funds.

IT'S ABOUT TIME

Does the congregation use time well? We are commanded by God to *redeem the time, for the days are evil.*[2] Services should start *on time*: we should not punish the punctual. Appointments should be kept, standards and priorities maintained. Immaturity in this area is a waste of one of our most precious resources.

CARE FOR PEOPLE

Are people appreciated for who they are? Are they appreciated for what they are willing to contribute of their time, talents and treasures? Are they well treated and cared for? This will be seen in the nursery, children's programs, ministering to single parents, and care for the elderly, poor and disabled in the fellowship. Yeshua taught us that what we do unto the least of His brethren we do unto Him.[3]

5) IS THE CONGREGATION'S LEADERSHIP DOMINATED BY THE LORDSHIP OF YESHUA?

This may be the most important question of all. Yeshua taught us that *if the blind lead the blind they all fall in a pit.*[4] What's the use of following a *shepherd* (pastor means shepherd) or the teaching of a teacher (rabbi means teacher) if he is not following the teaching himself?! We are all to *love the Lord our God with all our hearts and soul and might.*[5] Certainly the congregation leader is to model this for the fellowship. Being human, he may not always do so perfectly, but he is then to demonstrate the humility of repentance for the congregation.[6]

The Scriptures are clear on the leadership's spiritual qualifications[7] and responsibilities.[8] You should expect any congregation you join to have these same biblical standards. Take a moment to read the footnoted verses in your own Bible.

Questions
For your further study and consideration

Do you consiser the doctrinal position of a congregation to be important when considering a fellowship? Are there issues that are negotiable? Are there issues that are 'non-negotiable'? Why?

How can, or does, your congregation provide an opportunity for you to fulfill God's call for your life?

In what capacity are you presently serving your congregation?

FOOTNOTES

[1] see Ephesians 4:12, 15,16
[2] see Ephesians 5:16
[3] Matthew 25:40, 45
[4] Matthew 15:14
[5] Deuteronomy 6:5
[6] 1 Corinthians 11:1
[7] see 1 Timothy 3:1-12
[8] see Acts 6:4

Chapter Six

Confessing The Faith ...Wisely

I WILL TELL OF THY NAME TO MY BRETHREN;
IN THE MIDST OF THE ASSEMBLY
I WILL PRAISE THEE.
— David
Psalm 22:22

THE FRUIT OF THE RIGHTEOUS
IS A TREE OF LIFE,
AND HE WHO IS WISE WINS SOULS.
— Solomon
Proverbs 11:30

Sharing your faith is part of your living, growing spiritual relationship in the Lord. The 'vertical' aspects of your relationship with God are prayer and Scripture.

Regarding prayer, comedian Lily Tomlin asks the question, "Why is it when we say 'we talk to God' we call it *prayer*, but when we say 'God talks to us', they call it *insanity*?"

Though this may arouse a chuckle, the fact is God desires to have a real, two-way relationship with His people—where we talk to Him, and He speaks to us. *"My sheep hear My voice, and I know them, and they follow Me."*[1] In prayer we speak to God, and as we read the Scriptures, God speaks to each of us.

The 'horizontal' areas, relationships with people, are fellowship and sharing your faith. Fellowship is when you relate to people within the body of Messiah. Sharing your faith is your relating to people outside the body of Messiah. Sharing your faith is also known as "witnessing", "testifying" or "attesting."

In fact believers in Yeshua have not only the power but also the same God-given responsibility to let others know the Good News. For Yeshua said in Matthew 10:32,33...

> *Whoever will confess Me before men, I will also confess that person before My Father who is in heaven. But whoever will deny Me before men, I will also deny that person before My Father who is in heaven.*

Just as you might expect your spouse or even a good friend to introduce you to acquaintances and not to be ashamed of you, Messiah also expects those who have trusted in Him to acknowledge Him, and to be unashamed of Him. If you have at least confessed Him to somebody,

Mazel Tov! You're off to a good start! But—your family and friends need to know as well.

God doesn't give a believer responsibility without first giving him the power to fulfill that responsibility. The New Covenant teaches that all believers are especially enabled by the Holy Spirit to share the faith as His witnesses.

> *But you will receive power when the Holy Spirit has come upon you; and you will be my witnesses in Jerusalem, in all Judea and Samaria, and to the ends of the earth* (Acts 1:8).

It is of vital spiritual importance, as well as a matter of integrity, that believers share their faith and let their friends and families know what has happened to them. The longer it takes for them to tell their family and friends the more difficult the issue becomes. Don't lose heart, there are some wise ways to confess your faith.

WISELY BREAKING THE NEWS

First, when sharing your story, it is a good idea that the first person you break the news to not be the most uptight member of the family. Rather, consider an aunt, cousin, sister or parent that would be able to receive the news without *plotzing*, that is, fainting. Then ask that person for advice on how to approach other family members. If their response is, "Why do you have to tell anyone?", answer them by saying, "I have nothing to hide and I would rather have them hear it from me." Secondly, it is also wise to break it to them slowly. Let them know that you have been reading the Scriptures, and how the Bible seems to make a great deal of sense to you. Tell them you are praying regarding the issues you have read about in the Bible, particularly how it speaks very seriously about sin. Then speak to them about how the Scriptures present Messiah dying for our sins in portions like Isaiah 53, Daniel 9:26, Psalm 22 and others (see chart on page 191).

In any case, a gradual approach gets them to realize that your faith is something with thoughtful, careful consideration and substance, rather than merely believing something on a whim.

WISELY MEETING WITH THE RABBI

Amazingly, many Jewish families may want their adult children who believe in Yeshua to meet with a rabbi, even when it may have never seemed relevant to talk with a rabbi at any other time. Remember, as an adult you're under no obligation to meet with a rabbi, psychiatrist, or anyone else. You have done nothing morally wrong, and it's not crazy to believe in Yeshua. No one has the right to manipulate or force you to meet with anyone.

If you do decide to meet with the rabbi, don't feel concerned about needing to have technical biblical answers to his or her questions. If the rabbi asks you a question you can't answer, simply say, "I don't know, but I'll find out if you're really interested." We at Word of Messiah Ministries will be glad to provide any information you need in this regard. If you feel you aren't adequately prepared to share your faith with the rabbi, please contact us for the discipleship materials to help you grow in the Lord. This way you will be able to give an answer *"for the hope that is within you."*[2] Be prepared to discuss with your congregation leader your meeting with the non-Messianic rabbi. You may receive very helpful feedback and encouragement. Remember too, that the Scripture says, *"Greater is He that is in you than he that is in the world."*[3] You are not alone. You have the Person and power of *Ruach HaKodesh*, the Holy Spirit, living within you. Besides that, if you've been growing as a believer for a while, the rabbi may address areas that are actually more familiar to you than they are to him. So go easy on the rabbi, please! And always be polite and courteous.

WISELY EARN THE RIGHT TO BE HEARD...
...AND BELIEVED

It may seem to many in your family that it is the height of arrogance for you to appear to be telling your parents right from wrong. You are to *honor you father and mother*. It's especially absurd if you can't clean your room or keep a job, but you consider yourself qualified to explain eternal mysteries to them. It is better to earn the right to be heard by showing the new life you now have by faith in Messiah Yeshua. So, clean up your room, and get a job—and keep it. Whether your family realizes it or not, you are now the kind of child (or sister or brother) that they always wanted to have, because now you are dedicated to their welfare and eternal good.

At times, your family may caution you with a warning, "You can come to the party only if you promise not to talk about 'you-know-who'!" Beware of these manipulative actions and attitudes. You should never promise anyone that you will not talk about Messiah, since you already promised Him that you would, that is, as the proper occasion presents itself. All you can say to your family is that you will do nothing unbecoming.

If you have children be sure they understand that it is okay to speak freely about Yeshua, particularly when grandparents or relatives come to visit. To caution your children to not mention Yeshua around family members is to send the wrong message—that there is something wrong with believing in Yeshua. By doing so, you risk teaching them to hide the Good News from those who need to hear it most. Actually, sometimes the most powerful witness comes from a loving child, speaking simply and sincerely about the love of God.[4]

The best testimony is that you take your faith seriously, that it positively impacts your family, and that you are not ashamed of Messiah. Therefore, rather than not going to worship at all when your family is visiting, invite them to services with you. If your family declines the invitation, that's fine. Let them know you'll be back in a couple of hours. They will at least understand that your faith is vital to your life and your children's lives.

The Issue of Guilt

There are many Jewish believers who have a sense of guilt because of their faith in Yeshua—"Oh, I've broken my mother's heart." These guilty feelings are understandable, even if they are unfounded. Your family members' reaction to your faith is actually their responsibility, not yours. They need to accept you for who you are, even as you are to accept and love them unconditionally, regardless of their issues. Remember, Yeshua *is* the Jewish Messiah, and He will help you to be a better son or daughter now more than ever. In my own case this proved to be true. My father was quite hurt by my faith in Yeshua, but over the years he saw my life, and eventually recognized that Yeshua made me into a *mensch*—a man of character and worthy of respect. He even asked me to be the executor of his will!

The Issue of Authroity

Some adult Messianic believers might think that since the Scriptures teach us to "*Honor our father and mother*"[5] we therefore need to obey our parents in regards to our faith in Yeshua. One young Jewish man mistakenly did this. His father, who was not a believer, told him to get rid of the Bible, stop going to fellowship, and to stop praying. So he did, and he forsook following the Lord for a long, miserable period of time. (He later repented, and is today an elder in a Messianic congregation.) How, then, are we to understand our relationship to the various authority figures around us?

There are five areas of authority the Scriptures establish for the proper running of society that we need to be aware of and responsive to. These five areas are:

- ✡ *Parents to children*—Exodus 20:12; Ephesians 6:1
- ✡ *Husbands to wives*—Genesis 3:16; Ephesians 5:22-24, 1 Corinthians 11:2, 3
- ✡ *Elders to congregants*—Deuteronomy 18:18-19; Jeremiah 7:25, 26; Hebrews 13:17; 1 Peter 5:5
- ✡ *Employers to employees*—Psalm 123:2; 1 Peter 2:18;1 Timothy 6:1,2
- ✡ *Governors to citizens*—1 Samuel 24:6; Romans 13:1; 1 Peter 2:13,14

Anytime anyone in authority asks us to do that which God has forbidden, we must respectfully decline. The guiding principle in these matters is found in Acts 5:29, *We must obey God rather than man.* Therefore, if a husband asks his wife to sign a tax statement that is dishonest, she must respectfully decline; for the Scripture commands us not to steal—even from the government (Romans 13:6-8). If the boss asks an employee to lie for him, the employee must respectfully decline—the Scripture commands us not to lie.

Therefore if a family member asks us to disobey or even deny Messiah Yeshua, we cannot obey them, and must respectfully decline. The Scripture commands us to believe on and confess the Lord Yeshua.

Though obeying parents completely is for small children,[6] remember that you are still to honor your father and mother all the days of your life, even in honoring their memory after their passing.

For now, let them see that your love for them is even more dynamic because of the love of Yeshua in your heart—for no one loves your family as much as Messiah does.

QUESTIONS
FOR YOUR FURTHER STUDY AND CONSIDERATION

Have you shared your testimony with anyone yet? Why, or why not? If yes, how recently? How did the listener respond?

What do you consider the biggest obstacle people encounter regarding sharing their faith with others? Why?

Why is it important to earn the right to be heard?

FOOTNOTES
[1] John 10:27
[2] 1 Peter 3:15
[3] 1 John 4:4
[4] see Matt. 21:15,16, Luke 10:21
[5] Exodus 20:12
[6] Ephesians 6:1

Chapter Seven

Messianic Marriage and Dating

And Adam said:
"This is now bone of my bones
And flesh of my flesh;
She shall be called Woman,
Because she was taken out of Man."
Therefore a man shall leave his father
and mother and be joined to his wife,
and they shall become one flesh.
Genesis 2:23,24

Wives, submit to your own husbands,
as to the Lord.
Husbands, love your wives,
just as Messiah
also loved the congregation,
and gave Himself for her.
— Rabbi Shaul (Paul)
Ephesians 5:22,25

You Can Make It!

The highest and most sacred of human relationships is that of marriage. Marriage was, and *still is,* God's idea. Unfortunately, today marriages are failing to survive at an alarming rate. Over 50% of all marriages, including those of "believers", are ending in divorce. Certainly the majority of couples who stand at the altar before God and man have every intention of living in love "till death do us part." What has gone wrong? Is the institution of marriage itself flawed, or outdated? Is there a way to keep it together and make a marriage last in a world that seems to be hostile to the very ideals of fidelity, loyalty, and truth? The Bible says emphatically—Yes! You *can* win in the arena of holy matrimony, and have a marriage that not only survives, but thrives in the power and love of God!

"Feelings... Nothing More than Feelings?"

For many it may seem that the basis of marriage is *feelings* of love for the other person. However, the Bible teaches that strong and lasting marriages are based on the *truth* of love. Though the marriage relationship includes sexual pleasure, marriage is not based merely on its sexual aspect. Biblically, love is a 100% commitment to the eternal welfare of the other person.

Many couples can also get caught up in marital one-upsmanship. The joke is told: *"Last night I had my my wife on her knees! Of course at the time she was saying to me, 'Come out from under the bed and fight like a man!'"* Marriage can be frustrating, particularly when you expect the other person to meet all of your needs. It's like two fleas looking at each other, hoping the other one is the dog!

The marriage relationship is based on a couple's *spiritual* union in the Lord, and the secret for that union is a firm foundation in Messiah!

A Firm Foundation

Of all the things Yeshua taught us, one of the most fundamental principles is for us to live our lives founded on the truth of His word:

> *Therefore whosoever heareth these sayings of mine, and doeth them, I will liken him unto a wise man, which built his house upon a rock: and the rain descended, and the floods came, and the winds blew, and beat upon that house; and it fell not: for it was founded upon a rock. And every one that heareth these sayings of mine, and doeth them not, shall be likened unto a foolish man, which built his house upon the sand: And the rain descended, and the floods came, and the winds blew, and beat upon that house; and it fell: and great was the fall of it* (Matthew 7:24-27).

To attempt to live independently from God and His truth is like building a house on sand. No wise, thinking person would ever do this. However, the divorce epidemic is a sad testimony that people are essentially 'flying by the seat of their pants' through life, and consequently marriages are taking quite a beating. Recognizing that marriage is God's idea, it's a good idea to acquire His counsel on the matter. Or as the saying goes, "If all else fails, read the instructions."

GOD'S VIEWPOINT

In God's ultimate purpose for marriage we find the meaning of marriage for our own lives. God designed marriage above every other relationship to represent His own relationship with His people of faith. We are thus charged to relate to our spouses the way God relates to us. How does He relate to us, and what does He provide for your marriage relationship?

The Hebrew Bible in Genesis 2:24 gives us the relationship secret, "*A man shall <u>leave</u> father and mother and <u>cleave</u> to the spouse: and the two shall become <u>one</u> flesh.*" We find this basic tenet of marriage reiterated in the New Covenant with further insight:

> *For this cause shall a man leave his father and his mother, and shall be joined unto his wife, and the two shall be one flesh. This is a great mystery, but I speak concerning Messiah and the Congregation* (Eph. 5:31,32).

Marriage is a picture of our relationship with God. The two shall be one! But what does it take to attain oneness, or unity? Each spouse needs to *leave* and *cleave* to *achieve* unity.

YOU NEED TO... LEAVE

Leave father and mother. This does not mean to stop loving or honoring your family, but letting go of the emotional, psychological, and even spiritual attachments of your premarital life.

Ahzav עָזַב in Hebrew is a strong word meaning *to forsake*. Leaving the strong bond of premarital life means forsaking all others, refusing to bond with anyone or anything other than your spouse.

You can no longer be married to your job, your car, or to your computer! Whatever you 'cleaved' to in your previous life—LEAVE it!

Getting married and *leaving* is somewhat like the old job you left for a new one. You don't need to badmouth the old job, you may even speak honorably about it. So also with your parents: continue to honor them, but you're no longer bound to them.

When you get married, your loyalty, affection, zeal, and primary commitments have changed forever! This commitment is a reflection of your spiritual life. You cannot trust in Yeshua and continue to trust in other so-called gods: money, power, prestige, etc. God tolerates no competitors. The reason people don't follow God is because they have their own contingency plans, hedge their bets, and cover their bases.

In the same way a weak marriage has its prenuptial agreements and the like, instead of trusting in God and His wisdom. If you can see marriage is Biblically pictured as a relationship between Messiah and the Congregation, you must leave your bonding of the past and cleave, adhere, be joined to your own spouse. The problem Israel had during the Exodus was that though they left Egypt, Egypt didn't leave them. They lusted for the past. They held to the gods of the past. They needed to forget what was behind in order to press on to what was ahead! Have you left the past in the past? If you haven't, repent, and turn away from any other relationship that competes with your marriage.

You need to...Cleave
You are joined for the Lord

Cleave unto your wife. In truth, you leave to cleave! The Hebrew *davak*, דָּבַק, means *"to adhere, join, stick together."* The spiritually committed couple is joined *for* the Lord. They have a single-minded spiritual purpose in life. We can understand this idea of cleaving better as we see how the Bible uses *davak* elsewhere. This word is found in Daniel 2:43 where it is translated *adhere—"They will not adhere as iron is mixed with clay."* When a couple marries, they are like iron and clay: two different, incompatible substances. Substantial differences would normally prevent the cleaving process from occurring, but as a foundation of faith, common values and purity is established, these once 'incompatable substances' become one in the Lord. Amos 3:3 asks, *"How can two walk together unless they are in agreement?"* The couple that is of one mind in the Lord is growing in togetherness. Are you at odds with your spouse over these matters? Do you both agree that Yeshua is Lord of your marriage? If not, you are missing the key to genuine unity in your marriage relationship.

Though the goal of marriage is spiritual unity, this doesn't mean that you will be exactly alike either. Obviously females will remain females, and males will remain males. We're talking about unity, not uniformity. This means we are to accept one another as the Lord has accepted each of us.[1]

We are to cease trying to change one another into what we think our spouse should be, or even into our own image. Simply put, stop playing God! Each of you have your own job description. The Lord, the One to whom you each have to answer, has given them to us. For the wife it's found in Ephesians 5:22–24, and for the husband, 5:25–30. So stop bossing each other around; you already have a boss—the Lord Himself.

You are joined to the Lord

In cleaving, a couple has power for a godly purpose. Where is this 'cleaving power' found? In Psalm 63:8 the word *davak* is translated *clings*: "*My soul clings to you; Your right hand upholds me.*" When we know the Lord, we cleave to Him—holding onto His strong right hand. God's right hand—symbolic of His strength—can uphold your life and your marriage, and He is able to empower your marriage to fulfill His purposes.

How does a busy couple find the strength and power to live in unity, faith and love? Vince Lombardi, the legendary NFL coach once said, "Fatigue makes cowards of us all." Though life can wear us out, the Lord provides power to live for all who cling to one another in Him. Messiah is the key to the lasting bond for unity in marriage.

You are joined with the Lord

In cleaving there is real security in the Savior. Can you drift? We are not perfect people, just people. Even the best can fail.

Where is the security when we are weak, frail, and helpless? In Proverbs 18:24 the word *davak* is translated *sticks closer—There is a friend who sticks closer than a brother.* The word friend in Hebrew is *achav*, and means *the One who loves our souls*. There is a Friend Who *cleaves* to you, our Friend, Messiah Yeshua. When we are weak, He is stronger still! He is the security for our salvation and our marriages. For we know that *"nothing can separate us from the love of God in Yeshua HaMashiach Adoneinu—Yeshua the Messiah our Lord."*[2] There are many Goliaths, but we know One who is bigger, our God who promises He *"will never leave us nor forsake us."*[3] He will bring us through—if only we will trust in, and cleave to Him! Then our unity in marriage will be the picture of our relationship with God. Do you believe this? Faith is the victory!

In Unity there's a Personal relationship

God created people to be in an eternal and personal relationship with Himself. This committed relationship to God is the basis for our committed relationship to each other. Adam and Eve, the first married couple, strayed from this committed relationship with God, and through sin, that relationship with Him was broken. But God, being rich in mercy, promised that Messiah would come to be the atonement for our sins, and restore us to Himself. *For God so loved the world that he gave* Messiah that we might have life in Him, and personally know Him.

So also, in marriage it isn't a matter of mere vows and rules, but of intimate concern, caring and compassion for the other person. When one hurts, the other hurts; when one rejoices, both rejoice. It says of our God *"In all our afflictions He was afflicted."*[4] Messiah Yeshua died for your sins and was raised from the dead to prove it was all true. So through Messiah's atonement we have reconciliation with Him, and a living personal relationship with one another. Many marriages start off this way but then fail. What do you do when there is failure, disappointment, and hurt? We are charged to love and care for each other, reflecting God's love and care for us. You can't give what you haven't got. But in Messiah, we have the resource of forgiveness, kindness, and compassion, that we may minister and care for each other.

IN UNITY THERE'S A PRIORITIZED RELATIONSHIP

What is God doing? God's chief work is *you*; and His chief concern is your eternal welfare.[5] *You* are God's priority! Messiah died for you, and through His atonement He cleanses, fills and sets you apart unto Himself. Think about it. God prioritized your salvation over Messiah's life. So also in your relationship with your spouse there is to be priority and commitment to each other over every other friendship, or any other family tie.

If one night your husband is late for dinner, you can safely say, "Well whatever he's doing he's doing it for me." You are his chief priority this side of heaven.

And sir, you are her chief priority as well. Therefore you both are charged to re-prioritize your lives—forsaking all others and setting each other apart—because marriage is a prioritized relationship.

In Unity There's a Permanent Relationship

God has done so much to bring you to Himself in Messiah that Scripture says He will never leave you nor forsake you, and that nothing can separate you from the love of God in Messiah Yeshua. So in your union there's a permanence not based on mere human strength, nor hindered by human frailty, but a unity based on the forgiveness and acceptance you can have for each other in Messiah's atonement and grace.

A Three-fold Cord

True and lasting oneness necessitates the couple trusting daily in Yeshua. Like a braid of hair—though made up of three strands, it appears to contain only two. However, it is impossible to create a braid with only two strands. If you try to put the two together, they will quickly unravel. Herein lies the mystery: what looks like two strands requires a third. That third strand, though not immediately evident, keeps the braid tightly woven. Messiah's presence in a biblical marriage is the needed 'third strand', holding the wife and husband together, though to all casual observers it only appears as two!

Shema Yisrael Adonai Eloheinu Adonai Echad—Hear O Israel the Lord is our God the Lord is one.

Even as our God is permanently One, so also He declares in marriage *V'Ha'ya L'Va'sar Echad* וְהָיוּ לְבָשָׂר אֶחָד—*The two shall be one flesh.* In His unique *Echad/oneness*[6] is your unique oneness as well. In light of this, our Messiah declares about marriage, *"What God has joined together let no man separate."*[7] Therefore you are charged to commit yourself to grow into the experience of unity even as you are one in Messiah.

Has the Fire Gone Out?

What makes the difference in married lives is a couple's sincere dedication to Messiah for their marriage unity. A blacksmith once tried to unite two pieces of iron, but hammering all he could, they still would not become one. He then realized that he had forgotten what he should never have forgotten—the fire. Upon placing them in the fire, he found they could be easily melded together. Has the fire gone out of your marriage? Has the fire gone out in your relationship with the Lord? Has the fire of the Spirit yet melted your cold, iron hearts? If you will yield to the Lord, He will work in you heart, and your spouse's, that in Him the two of you may be one.

Take daily, personal time to be alone with God in prayer and study of His word.[8] Soon you will discover that His fire is once again burning brightly within, and this will kindle genuine intimacy in your relationship. As Messiah is exalted in your life, your marriage will enjoy all the blessings of God, and will be a blessing to others. And, let's face it, there's no where else to turn for blessings, for the Scripture declares that in Messiah are all the blessings of heaven.[9] Therefore trust the Lord, and work at it. Develop this wonderful relationship that pictures Messiah's own relationship with His people.

DEALING WITH IRRITATIONS

At the marriage altar, it may seem hard to believe that there will come a time when even the most godly and committed couple will have conflict, misunderstandings, and just plain irritate one another. What do we do? First, pray.

1) The Scripture encourages each of us to *cast your cares (anxieties) upon the Lord, because He cares for you.*[10] Bring your frustrations, hurts, and fears to God first. Let Him be your 'burden bearer.'

2) Recognize that you *are complete in Messiah,*[11] fully accepted in Yeshua, and that your life is not determined by your concerns, but by His *grace in which you stand.*[12]

3) Then by that very grace, and by relying on the power of *Ruach HaKodesh* (the Holy Spirit) recognize that you are uniquely called to minister to, and to love your spouse. Commit yourself in the Lord to care about that person. You will not be able to *meet all* your spouse's needs—only God can do that. But by Messiah's grace you can *minister* to your spouse's needs. This is walking by faith[13] in the newness of life,[14] as it relates to your marriage.

SHOULD A BELIEVER MARRY A NON-BELIEVER?

Though alluded to earlier let us now carefully consider the Scripture in this matter. We read in 2 Corinthians:

> *Do not be bound together with unbelievers; for what partnership has righteousness and lawlessness, or what fellowship has light with darkness? Or what harmony has Messiah with Belial, or what has a believer in common with an unbeliever? Or what agreement has the temple of God with idols? For we are the temple of the living God; just as God said, "I will dwell in them and walk among them; and I will be their God, and they shall be My people. Therefore, come out from their midst and be separate," says the Lord, "and do not touch what is unclean; and I will welcome you. And I will be a father to you, And you shall be sons and daughters to Me," says the Lord Almighty* (6:14-18).

The Scriptures teach that believers are not to marry—*not be bound together with*—non-believers. Why? Because there will be divided, even conflicting values and beliefs in the marriage. Though some have foolishly thought, "Well maybe my beloved will come to believe in Messiah after the marriage," in many cases, the marriage is weakened and the believing spouse becomes quite unhappy. In one situation, a young lady wanted to marry her unbelieving fiancé. At one of our Bible studies he came to faith in Messiah. As the wedding day approached, he became troubled, and asked me, "Sam, how can I marry someone who was willing to marry an unbeliever?" Oy! After some study and discipleship with both of them, this was eventually resolved and they were soon married.

All that said, we are to be faithful to the Lord and not compromise our testimony in Him. The best course of action to take is—don't even date, much less marry, an unbeliever.

WHAT IF I'M ALREADY MARRIED TO AN UNBELIEVER?

If you are already married to an unbeliever, the Scripture is clear on this point as well.

> *But to the rest I say, not the Lord, that if any brother has a wife who is an unbeliever, and she consents to live with him, he must not divorce her. And a woman who has an unbelieving husband, and he consents to live with her, she must not send her husband away*
> (1 Corinthians 7:12,13).

In other words, stay and win him or her to faith in Messiah by your dedicated love and kindness to them.[15] Yes, go to fellowship meetings, but not if it will break up your home. Some believers have had it very rough trying to live with insensitive, unbelieving spouse. As one person put it, "it's like living in prison." In other cases the unbelieving spouse is quite gracious, and permits the believer to enjoy his or her liberty in Messiah for worship and fellowship.

Similarly, the believer must be careful of tithing family money. The unbelieving spouse may resent you "giving away our hard-earned money to charity." Because every situation is different, and involves varying personalities, etc., your congregation leader may be able to give you more specific counsel on these matters.

SHOULD A JEWISH BELIEVER MARRY A GENTILE BELIEVER?

If God brings you together, then yes, absolutely! The Scriptures give liberty for any believer to marry any other believer,[16] but, there are still some issues to be wisely considered before you stand under the *chuppa*.[17]

The existence of Jewish believers in Yeshua today is a living demonstration of the faithfulness of the God of Israel.[18] Biblically therefore, every Jewish believer has the responsibility to perpetuate the Jewish people as a testimony to the faithfulness of God. If the marriage *is* of God, the Gentile believer will understand their responsibility to not let the Jewish people end with their family. Rather, he or she will desire to make the godly commitment to sustain the remnant of God's Chosen people. As Ruth, who was a Gentile, said to her Jewish mother-in-law, Naomi, *"Your people shall be my people and your God shall be my God,"*[19] every Gentile should be able to declare the same to their Jewish spouse. This will mean a personal involvement in messianic matters, as well as a commitment to raise the children *as Jews*, in a Messianic Jewish frame of reference. Yes, to be sure the Gentile side of the family brings values to be appreciated, but this is never to outweigh God's priority and promises regarding the 'Messianic witness' of the Jewish people.

Culturally, there are issues—particularly *Jewish* issues—to be considered as well. These include holiday observances that might confuse or inconvenience a Gentile spouse. For example, the leaven question at Passover; the fasting question at Yom Kippur; special foods that come with so many of the holidays and are an intrinsic part of the observance. Besides this, there are the basic interests and concerns: understanding the need to support Israel, to stand against anti-Semitism, to become aware and sensitive to Jewish history and culture. These are matters that need to be discussed and understood through pre-marital counseling sessions with your congregation leader.

DATING

Whatever your age, whether you are 17 or 70, dating can be an enjoyable, though sometimes precarious experience. Why date at all? Many see dating as a fun time with no commitment to the other person, sort of "playing the field," as they say. Dating is actually a modern concept contrived by our Western culture. Though it is common practice in the West, in many parts of the world, to send one's daughter out with a young man without a chaperone is unimaginable. Moreover, though it is popular, dating simply isn't taught in the Scriptures.

In Biblical times, marriages were often arranged by parents, possibly including a period of supervised courtship. Though today this is considered to be old fashioned and archaic, it is thought that arranged marriages were actually more successful than marriages are today.

Additionally, 'safety precautions' such as group dating or chaperoned dating (by parents or responsible married couples) really are great ideas. It's very important to protect the reputation of the person you're on a date with. Of course we're always to remember that dating never includes sexual activity outside of marriage which the Bible strictly forbids. Bottom line, dating or courtship, is really a time to assess the "spouse potential" of the other person. Though people may be unduly drawn to their date's physical appearance, the key issue is to evaluate the person's *spiritual maturity*, and fitness for the married life.

OY VEY, I'M SINGLE!

One word of wisdom: do not be in a hurry. Even if you think 'life is passing you by', and 'all of the good ones are taken.' There are times we may think something like, "Oh no, I'm 24 and I'm not married *yet*!" Many bad decisions have been made out of a sense of desperation. Understand this: if you are single, God has called you to be single—at least *for today*. Yeshua, Who *has* called you, put it best: *"Therefore do not be anxious for tomorrow; for tomorrow will care for itself. Each day has enough trouble of its own."*[20]

IN GOD'S HANDS

Remembering how Joseph's trial of faith changed dramatically in the course of a single day[21], commit your situation to the safest possible place: God's hands.

He knows where you are, and He knows who He is preparing for you. Therefore, walk with the Lord *daily*; wait upon Him quietly in your devotional time. Remember, it's easier to get *into* a bad relationship than it is to *get out* of one, so let the Lord lead and encourage you, and wait for His perfect timing.[22]

SUITABLE FOR FRAMING

In general, when two believers do date they should be asking questions of each other to find out if there is genuine suitability for a long term and committed relationship. Since oneness is the goal, initial discussions should center on spiritual issues: your salvation experiences; spiritual victories and challenges; spiritual lifestyle issues, prayer and devotion schedules/habits; fellowship attendance and spiritual service, etc.

When there is spiritual compatibilty evidenced, then soul, or personality issues can be discussed. These include:

✿ intellectual ideas that reflect your values;
✿ emotional matters that gladden your heart or grieve your soul;
✿ goals and commitments you're persuing and seeking to accomplish in your life.

Then after you are married, and only after the wedding, can physical oneness be enjoyed together in the realization that the Lord has brought you together for life, and made you one in His love.

Who should do the marrying?

That depends on several issues. Legally of course, anyone qualified will do—the Justice of the Peace, or a ship's captain has served many in their time of need. But, if this is to be a marriage committed to the honor of God, then one would expect a minister of God to officiate.

Whether it is a Messianic minister or not depends on the commitments of the couple. Normally, they should be counseled pre-maritally, and married by the leader of the congregation where they are faithful members. Being faithful and involved in your congregation will provide the opportunity for encouargement and counselling after the wedding. Generally speaking, if you're not members of a congregation, you probably aren't ready for marriage.

Integrity Counts

Having a church or synagogue wedding when you're not committed to the Lord, and where you don't belong as a member, is simply a sham. This is the very hypocrisy that will undermine the integrity upon which all marriages depend. In marriage, it's substance, not symbolism, that counts.

Equally questionable is desiring a Messianic *wedding* without desiring a Messianic *marriage*. The relatives may be fooled at first, but a superficial messianic commitment will eventually undermine your testimony. If you really care about your testimony and your marriage, make yours a testimony of integrity. That integrity will give credibility to all you have to say about Messiah to your family. In other words, join a congregation that will support, and not contradict, your messianic testimony.

There are times that Messianic ministers are asked to perform the ceremony without mentioning *Messiah Yeshua* by name. Think about it: if you hide Him at the wedding, what makes you think you will reveal Him through the marriage? Such a request is usually made because of sensitivities for the unbelievers present—perhaps even for family members involved in the wedding party who may be uncomfortable, even incensed, with the whole Messiah Yeshua thing.

Despite sensitivities involved, it is inappropriate and disloyal for any Messianic leader to officiate at a wedding, or any other ceremony, without honoring that *"Name which is above every name, the name Yeshua."*[23] The only authority that a Messianic leader has to minister is from the Lord, in His Name—and that authority is given to proclaim the truth of the Good News.

MAZEL TOV!

Marriage is God's opportunity to demonstrate through your wedded relationship His kind of faithful love to the community. This is also your opportunity to grow in the love, grace and knowledge of God as you dedicate your relationship to reflect His love and goodness in your lives.

Therefore, with *chuppa* and *broken wine glass*[24], with *shevet berochot*[25] and *motzi*[26]—with all of this, and exalted above all of this, is Messiah! In Yeshua we find the only hope for a couple, their marriage, and for all of Israel as well. Start out on the right foot, and you'll be less likely to stumble spiritually as you follow Messiah in your marriage relationship.

Trust in the grace of Yeshua, and the light of His Word and the power of His Holy Spirit will enable you to live in spiritual victory day by day. Yours will be a marriage honoring to the Lord and lived out on earth for all to see—a marriage literally made in Heaven!

QUESTIONS
FOR YOUR FURTHER STUDY AND CONSIDERATION

As a single person, a parent, or a young person, what do you believe is the purpose of dating? Do you think that your views agree or disagree with God's viewpoint?

Why is it important for a believer in Yeshua to marry only another believer in Yeshua?

What does it mean for a person to 'leave and cleave', and do you think this is important? Why?

FOOTNOTES

[1] Romans 15:7
[2] Romans 8:39
[3] Joshua 1:9, Hebrews 13:5
[4] Isa. 63:9
[5] See John 3:16
[6] For more on God's unique *Echad,* see WMM books *"Growing in Messiah"* and *"The Messianic Answer Book"*
[7] Matt. 19:6
[8] See 1 Cor. 7:5
[9] See Eph. 1:3
[10] 1 Peter 5:7
[11] Col 2:10
[12] Romans 5:2
[13] 2 Corinthians 5:7
[14] Romans 6:4
[15] See also 1 Peter 3:1-7
[16] 1 Corinthians 7:39, 2 Cor. 6:14,15
[17] The *chuppa* is the canopy, sometimes consisting of a *tallit* (prayer shawl) suspended on four poles, under which the wedding ceremony is conducted.
[18] Romans 11:1-5
[19] Ruth 1:16
[20] Matt. 6:34
[21] Read Genesis 41
[22] Ecc. 3:11; Song of Solomon 2:7
[23] Philippians 2:9, 10
[24] Tradionally at the end of the marriage ceremony, the groom crushes a glass under his heel.
[25] *Shevet berochot* are the seven benedictions pronounced at traditional Jewish weddings.
[26] *Motzi* is the blessing pronounced over the bread.

Chapter Eight

Messianic Believers
and
Circumcision

This is My covenant, which you shall keep, between Me and you and your descendants after you: every male among you shall be circumcised. And you shall be circumcised in the flesh of your foreskin; and it shall be the sign of the covenant between Me and you. – God to Abraham
Genesis 17:10,11

Moreover the LORD your God will circumcise your heart and the heart of your descendants, to love the LORD your God with all your heart and with all your soul, in order that you may live.
– Moses
Deuteronomy 30:6

Though commanded in Torah, some sincere Jewish New Covenant believers wonder whether it is permitted to have a circumcision (called *Brit Milah*) performed on their newborn sons. Their confusion may result from Paul's teaching in Galatians that it is wrong to circumcise *Gentile* believers for them to be complete in the Lord.[1] As you will see, Paul, who forbade circumcision for Gentiles, at the same time expected Jewish males to be circumcised.

REMEMBER, GOD IS FAITHFUL

According to Torah, all male Jewish babies are to be circumcised on the eighth day. Please realize that having your son circumcised *does not* place your child "under the Law." In Acts 16:1-3 even Paul the Apostle circumcised Timothy for the sake of Timothy's testimony to the surrounding Jewish community. And what is that testimony? Not that I do this to *become* Jewish. But that "I do this because *I am* Jewish, and because Yeshua is the fulfillment, not the nullification of the Abrahamic Covenant[2], and the fulfillment of all the promises to Israel." Yeshua did not abrogate the Abrahamic Covenant that established circumcision as its sign. This also doesn't "save" the child, since circumcision doesn't save anyone anymore than infant baptism can save an infant.[3] Salvation is always by personal faith in Yeshua. Rather, circumcision is an outward reminder to your child that God is faithful to His people and of his need to give his heart to Messiah for *"the circumcision that is not made with hands."*[4]

Are we Under the Law?

So, why should Jewish believers in Yeshua have their male babies circumcised? I myself struggled over this when my son Joshua was about to be born. I had not been taught the biblical view, and was concerned that I might be putting my son under the law, or that I might be displeasing God in some way. After a thorough study on the subject I understood more clearly the scriptural picture of circumcision. It was a matter of my calling and testimony as a Jewish believer in Yeshua.

A Sign of the Abrahamic Covenant

Though circumcision was so often identified with the Law, it actually preceded the Torah. It was given as a sign of the Abrahamic Covenant: *"And you shall be circumcised in the flesh of your foreskin, and it shall be the sign of the covenant between Me and you."*[5] The Abrahamic Covenant was made up of a three-part promise:[6] (1) a land; (2) a seed; and (3) a blessing. *The land* included all and more of the geographical area of the present nation of Israel;[7] *the seed* promised the continued existence of the Jewish people and the line of kings coming from that seed;[8] and *the blessing* is ultimately manifested in the Messiah Yeshua for all who will believe.[9]

A Reminder of spiritual Hope

The Abrahamic Covenant was the hope of Israel.[10] When Israel sinned, in order to safeguard Israel, Moses pleads not the Torah, but the Abrahamic covenant before God.[11]

The Abrahamic covenant was a reminder of God's *unconditional promises* to the nation of Israel. Though the sign of the Abrahamic Covenant is circumcision,[12] the sign of circumcision was never a means of personal salvation. The people were reminded that having a circumcised heart for God is necessary for a personal relationship with God.

> *Moreover the LORD your God will circumcise your heart and the heart of your descendants, to love the LORD your God with all your heart and with all your soul, so that you may live* (Deuteronomy 30:6).
>
> *Circumcise yourselves to the LORD and remove the foreskins of your heart, men of Judah and inhabitants of Jerusalem, or else My wrath will go forth like fire and burn with none to quench it, because of the evil of your deeds* (Jeremiah 4:4).
>
> *But he is a Jew who is one inwardly; and circumcision is that which is of the heart, by the Spirit, not by the letter; and his praise is not from men, but from God.* (Romans 2:29).

Circumcision in and of itself meant nothing to God apart from a spiritually committed heart of faith.

> *"Behold, the days are coming," declares the LORD, "that I will punish all who are circumcised and yet uncircumcised—Egypt and Judah, and Edom and the sons of Ammon, and Moab and all those inhabiting the desert who clip the hair on their temples; for all the nations are uncircumcised, and all the house of Israel are uncircumcised of heart"* (Jer. 9:25,26; see also Acts 7:51).

A Testimony of Hope in God

Therefore all Jewish males were circumcised to testify to their hope in the Abrahamic covenant and the faithfulness of God—even Yeshua:

And when eight days had passed, before His circumcision, His name was then called Yeshua, the name given by the angel before He was conceived in the womb (Luke 2:21).

Paul was falsely accused of teaching Jewish believers not to circumcise their infant boys:

But they have been informed about you that you teach all the Jews who are among the Gentiles to forsake Moses, saying that they ought not to circumcise their children nor to walk according to the customs (Acts 21:21).

From Paul's point of view, an uncircumcised Jewish believer was, in fact, a detriment to ministry for Yeshua—and it bears repeating—Yeshua is not the nullification, but the fulfillment of the Abrahamic covenant, and the very hope of Israel. This is why Paul circumcised Timothy before allowing him to go into service for Messiah:

Paul wanted this man to go with him; and he took him and circumcised him because of the Jews who were in those parts, for they all knew that his father was a Greek (Acts 16:3).

All Jewish believers in Yeshua have a responsibilty to maintain a present tense Jewish identity. But with that responsibility, they have liberty regarding how their Jewish identity is expressed. We read in Colossians 2:16,17...

Therefore no one is to act as your judge in regard to food or drink or in respect to a festival or a new moon or a Sabbath day—things which are a mere shadow of what is to come; but the substance belongs to Messiah.

No one is to judge another Jewish believer in matters of Jewish identity: whether it be what foods we eat, or what festivals we celebrate. This has to do with how we understand the calling of God in our lives, as regarding our Messianic witness to the Jewish community around us.

But, just as it is right for Jews to be circumcised in light of the Abrahamic promises fulfilled in Yeshua, it is wrong for Gentiles to be circumcised for spiritual/religious reasons; and Paul refused to allow it.

> *But not even Titus, who was with me, though he was a Greek, was compelled to be circumcised* (Gal. 2:3).

> *It was for freedom that Messiah set us free; therefore keep standing firm and do not be subject again to a yoke of slavery. Behold I, Paul, say to you that if you receive circumcision, Messiah will be of no benefit to you. And I testify again to every man who receives circumcision, that he is under obligation to keep the whole Law. You have been severed from Messiah, you who are seeking to be justified by law; you have fallen from grace. For we through the Spirit, by faith, are waiting for the hope of righteousness. For in Messiah Jesus neither circumcision nor uncircumcision means anything, but faith working through love* (Gal. 5:1-6).

A Picture of spiritual life in Yeshua

In Messiah we receive the true circumcision of the heart in order to have a right relationship with God—and Yeshua is the *Mohel,* or circumciser:

> *And in Him you have been made complete, and He is the head over all rule and authority; and in Him you were also circumcised with a circumcision made without hands, in the removal of the body of the flesh by the circumcision of Messiah* (Col. 2:10,11).

Therefore every Jewish believer should have their male children circumcised as a testimony to our hope in God. They should then pray diligently for their children to come to personal faith in Messiah. It is this spiritual circumcision of the heart that is necessary, and is received by faith in Yeshua for all who will believe, Jew or Gentile, male or female.

QUESTIONS
FOR YOUR FURTHER STUDY AND CONSIDERATION

Does having your son(s) circumcised place them under the demands of Torah? Why, or why not?

What three areas does the Abrahamic Covenant address?

What is God's ultimate purpose for the sign of circumcision? (See Deuteronomy 30:6).

FOOTNOTES

[1] Galatians 5:2,3
[2] Galatians 3:14
[3] see Jer. 9:24,25
[4] Col. 2:11
[5] Gen. 17:11
[6] Gen. 12:1-3
[7] Gen. 15:18
[8] Gen.15:4; 17:4-8
[9] see Galatians 3:14,16
[10] Deut. 7:7-9
[11] Ex. 32:13
[12] Genesis 17:9-14

Regarding the participation of Messianic believers in *Mikvah/Tavilah* (baptism) and *Zicharon* (the Lord's Supper, or Communion) see WMM's book *"Growing in Messiah: Vital truths for Growing Messianic Believers."*

Chapter Nine

Messianic Believers and Bar/Bat Mitzvah

It is common in traditional Jewish circles that after Bar/Bat Mitzvah, many children forsake religious involvement. So common, in fact, that this story is told of poor Rabbi Yossi in a poor synagogue that was infested with mice. Seeking advice to remedy this situation, Rabbi Yossi went to Rabbi Rosen, who said, "Oy, I tried poison but it didn't help." He then went to Rabbi Cohen who said, "Oy, I tried traps. But the mice were too smart to get caught!" Finally Yossi went to Rabbi Maven, who said, "I got rid of all my mice!" "Nu, How?!", a surprised Yossi asked. Rabbi Maven proudly explained, "I lined them up, taught them Hebrew, then made them all Bar Mitzvah—and they never showed up in my synagogue again!"

Though many may forsake spiritual pursuits after Bar Mitzvah, we expect better of our children and our *B'nai* Mitzvah* (*pronounced bə-nā`). Since we as Messianic believers are decidedly predisposed to Jewish cultural expression of the faith, we have various customs that may confuse some. Invariably, when Jewish customs are observed I can usually count on one of two responses. One response is "why do we have to do that; it's so legalistic." The other response is "anything Jewish is blessed."

THE MEANING OF BAR/BAT MITZVAH

The words *Bar* or *Bat Mitzvah* mean *Son, or Daughter of the Commandment,* respectively. Because of the word "commandment" there are some who would prefer another word like *hesed* (merciful love). Certainly this is an option, but what is gained by the change? since the New Covenant teaches disciples to keep all that Yeshua commanded.[1] In fact, obedience is evidence of our love for God.[2] So even under New Covenant authority we still have to deal with the issue of the commandments.[3]

Let's understand something about commandments. God lets us know His priorities for our lives by putting His truth in the imperative. We are not legalists for obeying His commands, rather, we're wise. When the Lord says "Do not steal," why don't we steal? Because *"the Lord is my Shepherd, I shall not want."*[4] Our behavior reflects upon Him. We can trust God and not dishonor Him by stealing.

This trust develops character and makes us into a people of conviction—the commandments of God are the convictions of the saints.

THE CONCEPT OF BAR/BAT MITZVAH

Bar Mitzvah is a challenge to the young person to become a spiritually mature adult. Though tradition declares the Bar Mitzvah to be an adult, this isn't really adulthood. In the Bible the age for adulthood was twenty. In war: *"from twenty years old and upward, whoever is able to go out to war in Israel"*;[5] also for giving contributions, *"Everyone who is numbered, from twenty years old and over, shall give the contribution to the LORD."*[6]

According to Jewish tradition, Bar Mitzvah is the inception of spiritual responsibilities. These include being responsible for one's own sins; being called to read Torah publically in synagogue; being allowed or expected to wear *tefillin*[7]; being qualified for an arranged marriage, and being responsible for keeping vows made.

Bar Mitzvah challenges children to grow during their passage into adolescence, and to mature with the approaching responsibilities of adulthood.

THE HISTORY OF BAR/BAT MITZVAH

Bar Mitzvah is not a biblical practice. Though it is not forbidden, neither is it mandated. Historically and as required by Torah, all young men would appear in Jerusalem for the appointed feast days.[8] During the Second Temple period, boys were customarily brought to Jerusalem for worship responsibilities at age 13, unless the child was deemed by a rabbi to be sufficiently mature at age 12. This may have been the case for Yeshua who was taken to the Temple when he was twelve years of age.[9] The vows of a 12-year-old boy were considered legally valid, but the boy had first to be examined for signs of physical maturity. The Talmud records this as a normative custom:

> The age at which a child has to be trained for his future responsibilities on attaining his majority. Normally eleven or twelve years of age (Sukkah 28b).

By the first century, the idea of maturity continued to develop. Boys of 13, and girls of 12, were considered marriageable, and religiously could be part of the worship community.

The actual ceremony that we identify as Bar Mitzvah was not referred to as such until the Middle Ages. A celebration was held for a religiously responsible, marriageable youth, during which the father would declare, "I'm no longer responsible for my son's sins." In the 18th century, the Reform Synagogue introduced confirmation at 16 years of age, thinking it a more reasonable age to consider a youth to be responsible. Although Bar Mitzvah remained more popular than confirmation, still today some Reform congregations do both. For girls, Bat Mitzvah was instituted in the 1900's.

More Than a Show

In many places Bar/Bat Mitzvah has now become a big show, and may actually have little to do with genuine spiritual commitments on anyone's part. For many Jewish believers the idea of having their child become Bar Mitzvah may be thought of as merely a time to show the relatives 'we're still Jewish.' Though your testimony is important, if the only motivation is for a showy 'witness', the act itself can become spiritually meaningless to the child. Such events are more like a dog and pony show, and the child's adolescent years may demonstrate the shallowness of such a view. Should not Bar Mitzvah be different for us? Yes it should.

Bar Mitzvah should communicate to the child the spiritual meaning and value of their Jewish identity in Messiah. Even if they have no relatives to consider, there are valid reasons to endure both the training for Bar Mitzvah and the terror of standing in front of a crowd. The value of Bar Mitzvah is for the child to publicly testify of their personal faith in God, and that they are dedicating themselves to the Lord. Bar/Bat Mitzvah is, in a real sense, the challenge of maturity for the child, and his or her parents.

SOME CONCERNS ABOUT BAR/BAT MITZVAH
1. By becoming a son of the commandment is the child taking on the obligation of the Law?
Not at all! The commandment with which the child is identifying is the Law of Messiah as found in 1 Corinthians 9:21: "[I became] *to those who are without law, as without law, though not being without the law of God but under the law of Messiah,"* and in Galatians 6:2, *"Bear one another's burdens, and thereby fulfill the law of Messiah."*

2. By practicing this ceremony are believers giving it spiritual implications that are not valid?

The only way to become a true Bar/Bat Mitzvah is through faith in Yeshua.[10] The ceremony itself is only an outward confirmation of an inward reality. Until they profess faith in Messiah, unbelieving children should not undergo Bar Mitzvah since they would deny the very truth they supposedly are submitting to.

3. Does Bar/Bat Mitzvah set up a dichotomy between Jewish and non-Jewish kids?

Actually, for Jewish and non-Jewish believers this is an excellent opportunity to show our unity in Messiah! Even though it is a Jewish custom, Bar Mitzvah is an excellent opportunity for Gentiles to recognize their faith in the God of Israel, their being 'grafted into the olive tree' as stated in Romans 11:17, and their love and appreciation for Jewish culture and heritage.

4. Should Gentile believers really have a Bar/Bat Mitzvah?

As a member of a Messianic congregation, all kids should be challenged to maturity and to dedicate their lives to Messiah. If this is the value, then it seems reasonable that any child may participate.

As Gentile believers, you do not want to confuse the issue by erroneously asserting that somehow Gentiles become Jewish. The ceremony does not make anyone Jewish, but can be seen as a rite of passage for young people desiring to live for the Lord.

Thus all Jewish *and* non-Jewish children can have a Bar/Bat Mitzvah, or a confirmation ceremony, which is a normal custom for Messianic congregations and fellowships. Gentile kids have just as much right as Jewish kids to 'suffer' through Bar Mitzvah.

THE PRACTICE OF BAR/BAT MITZVAH
THE OVERARCHING PRINCIPLE

Messianic Bar/Bat Mitzvahs must be 'Messiah centered': Yeshua is to be exalted in all things, by all people, for all time.

THE OPERATING PROCEDURE

The Bar Mitzvah should have *biblically relevant liturgy* that is more than mere *performance*, rather it is a *testimony* of faith.

There should be Messiah-oriented readings such as Isaiah 7:14; 9:6; 11:1-3; 53, etc. Other portions, of course, can be used (i.e., the weekly portion in the traditional yearly reading schedule), but effort should be exerted to focus attention upon Messiah.[11]

As part of his or her presentation, the child should give a testimony of personal faith in Yeshua and a *drash* (comment) on the Scriptures. Thanks to the parents and teachers should be expressed, and most of all, appreciation should be made to the Lord for His love, care and help.

There should be a clarification of what the event means, especially for non-Jewish children going through Bar Mitzvah, and non-Jewish visitors. Again, no one should think we are declaring Gentile children to be Jewish.

The Value of Bar/Bat Mitzvah

✡ *Spiritually*—it is a time to clarify and consecrate the child and their dedication to follow and grow in the Lord.

✡ *Culturally*—it is an opportunity for identification with our people. This has become an important cultural milestone in the life of any Jewish young person.

✡ *Emotionally*—it is a bridge to adulthood. There are increased privileges and responsibilities.

✡ *Instructionally*—it is an opportunity for:
Family—will hear of the child's faith in a culturally sensitive context. Some unsaved family members will come to a Bar Mitzvah who otherwise would not darken the doorway of a Messianic congregation.
Friends—It provides natural setting for the child to share their faith and commitment to the Lord with unsaved friends.

The Biblical Values of Bar/Bat Mitzvah

Inasmuch as Bar Mitzvah challenges our children to maturity, it reflects truths such as those found in Isaiah 7:15,16, which discusses a spiritual 'rite of passage' for a young person:

> He will eat curds and honey at the time He knows to refuse evil and choose good. For before the boy will know to refuse evil and choose good, the land whose two kings you dread will be forsaken (Isaiah 7:15,16).

Isaiah teaches there comes a point when people are held responsible before God for their choices in life. We call this "the age of accountability." Prior to this time children are not held responsible.

Therefore when babies die we understand they go to heaven[12] (this also applies to the severely retarded). Deuteronomy 1:37-40 speaks of God's judgment on the people of Israel who, because of their rebellion against the Lord, were barred from the Promised Land. In this situation the Lord says, *"And the little ones that you said would be taken captive, your children who do not yet know good from bad— they will enter the land."* It's not that small children do not commit sins, it's just that the Scriptures do not hold them morally responsible, for they have not come to a place where they can *refuse the evil and choose the good*.

Among ancient Jews, what came to be called Bar Mitzvah signaled an age of accountability— going from being a child, a minor, to entering into adulthood. Not that kids at this age had all the rights and responsibilities of full-grown adults, but it was recognized that they could now make certain moral choices in their lives. Exactly what the age of accountability is for each individual, no one can easily say. There are some kids that seem to know 'what's cooking' from 6 or 7 years of age, and there are others that even at 40 don't know the score.

We see the general Jewish overview of the chronological milestones in the Talmud...[13]

> He used to say: five years is the age for the study of scripture, ten-for the study of Mishnah, <u>thirteen for becoming subject to commandments</u>, fifteen for the study of Talmud, eighteen for the bridal canopy, twenty for pursuing/war, thirty for full strength, forty for understanding, fifty for ability to give counsel,

sixty-for mature age, seventy for a hoary head, eighty is a sign of super-added strength, ninety is the age for a bending figure, at a hundred, one is as one that is dead, having passed and ceased from the world.

MATURITY ASSUMES COMPREHENSION OF GOOD AND EVIL

As our children make the transition from childhood to adulthood, what are they learning from our own lifestyles? Are they learning right from wrong? Have *you* learned right from wrong? Many of us haven't, and think that ignorance is bliss—but spiritual naiveté is spiritual immaturity. Some of us choose to live according to the so called 'wisdom' of the world—might makes right; I don't get mad, I get even; rules are made to be broken; God helps those that help themselves; it's dog eat dog; etc. Will we live under the influence of the world's sin, cynicism, and materialism, or will we live in genuine trust and faith in God? However we choose to live, it is very likely that our children will follow in our footsteps.

"For before the boy will know to refuse evil and choose good...", but what is good according to Isaiah? Good is not merely what is good for oneself, but what is good from God's eternal perspective and reflects His heart and nature—for *"the Lord is good."*[14] This means there *are* principles God wants us to choose to live by that further His plans and honor His Name, and He wants us to refuse the evil that will dishonor Him. Do you know that there are moral absolutes that you need to heed? These will determine your

fulfillment in life as surely as the absolute need you have for air, food, and water. The Scriptures not only teach us *what* these absolutes are, but *how* to instruct our children to choose the good, and refuse the evil.

MATURITY ASSUMES THERE ARE CONSEQUENCES FROM GOOD AND EVIL CHOICES

It is possible to have knowledge of good and evil, and still not realize our choices make an intrinsic difference. It's not what you *know*, but what you *sow*, that you will reap. Sow orange seeds and you don't reap apples. Sow hate and you don't receive love. Sow unbelief and you don't get trust. There are consequences to our choices, as the Scripture says, *"be sure your sin will find you out!"*[15] No one gets away with anything. Some do not understand the difference between *gratification of a lust* and the *satisfaction of a life*. As the Scripture says, *"For he who sows to his flesh will of the flesh reap corruption, but he who sows to the Spirit will of the Spirit reap everlasting life."*[16]

In the story of the rich man and Lazarus found in the ook of Luke,[17] a rich man lived extravagantly and thought it was irrelevant that he ignored the poor man, Lazarus, living right outside his door. The rich man's sin against God was manifested in his disregard of his fellow man, namely Lazarus. The rich man was condemned not merely by the evil he had *committed*, but by the righteousness he *omitted*.

Maturity Assumes Choosing Good over Evil

Indeed, it's not merely knowing, nor recognizing, but choosing good and refusing evil that the work of maturity is realized. Therefore children must be taught properly first, so they can make mature decisions. God has always expected His people to choose the good in order that He might bless us. Our faith is seen in our choices. Good choices = good faith. Bad choices = bad faith. Growth is not *discovering* yourself, but *developing* yourself. How? By making good, faithful choices, you and your children will mature into the kind of people God created you to be.

Maturity Assumes Commitment to Good and Not to Evil

While speaking to a group of quite wealthy people a minister, not wanting to offend them, proclaimed, "Repent of your sins!—more or less; Ask for forgiveness—in a measure, or you'll be damned—to some extent." Regarding moral issues, we know there is no middle ground, nor does the Bible teach us to compromise with evil.

✡ *If it is disagreeable in your sight to serve the LORD, choose for yourselves today whom you will serve: ...but as for me and my house, we will serve the LORD (Joshua 24:15).*

✡ *You cannot serve both God and Mammon (Matt. 6:24).*

✡ *He who would be friends with the world is an enemy of God (James/Jacob 4:4).*

✡ *Do not love the world nor the things in the world. The one who loves the world the love of the Father is not in him (1 John 2:15).*

✡ *By faith Moses, when he had grown up, refused to be called the son of Pharaoh's daughter, choosing rather to endure ill-treatment with the people of God than to enjoy the passing pleasures of sin, considering the reproach of Messiah greater riches than the treasures of Egypt; for he was looking to the reward (Hebrews 11:24-26).*

✡ *Elijah came near to all the people and said, "How long will you hesitate between two opinions? If the LORD is God, follow Him; but if Baal, follow him" (1 Kings 18:21).*

God's people have always had to choose one way or the other—to either follow God and the truth, or follow a sinful lie. You cannot be both spiritually mature and also live in sin. To live in sin is carnality and immaturity. You can't be both the people of the world and the people of God.[18] There's not one person that God called to immaturity.

Maturity is the only choice for the people of God as we press on to the mark of the high calling of God. Bar/Bat Mitzvah is the time to commit oneself to maturity in the Lord. *Choose this day whom you will serve.* Does this seem too radical? The heroes of the faith who turned the world upside down for Yeshua were those who would not compromise the truth. Refuse the evil, and choose the good. That's where our heroes will come from today and tomorrow. Those children and adults who respond to that challenge of maturity will declare along with Moses, Elijah, Paul and Joshua *"as for me and my house I will serve the Lord"*.[19]

God wants to help you to make right choices in your life. How does God help you to choose?

✡ By developing a reverent attitude towards God. *Who is the person who fears the LORD?*

He will instruct that one in the way he should choose (Psalm 25:12).
- By proper activity, study of God's word. *Let Your hand be ready to help me, for I have chosen Your precepts* (Psalm 119:173).
- By following His word. *I have chosen the faithful way; I have placed Your ordinances before me* (Psalm 119:30).
- By following godly examples. We are warned not to choose violent people to follow. *Do not envy a man of violence and do not choose any of his ways* (Proverbs 3:31). So consider **WWYD**? What would Yeshua do?

GOD'S GOAL: YOUR MATURITY

Maturity includes the issues of, and is evidenced by, completeness, wholeness, wisdom, and fullness of life. How does a person grow into these qualities? We must choose the good as opposed to the evil. But remember, the world we live in has for the most part rejected the truth of God and opted for a lie. The world has chosen the economy over character, symbolism over substance, trivia over truth. Understand the world cannot be your guide. In fact, our most important choice in life is to choose what the world has rejected: Messiah.

> *The stone which the builders REJECTED Has become the chief corner stone* (Psalm 118:22).
> *And coming to Him as to a living stone which has been REJECTED by men, but is choice and precious in the sight of God* (1 Peter 2:4).

By choosing Messiah you take your first step to true maturity, fulfillment, and wholeness, by coming into an eternal relationship with God!

QUESTIONS
FOR YOUR FURTHER STUDY AND CONSIDERATION

Name some of the benefits of having your child Bar/Bat Mitzvahed.

How can Bar/Bat Mitzvah help young people learn about one's commitment to honor and follow the God of Israel?

What can you as a parent do to help prepare your child, not only for Bar/Bat Mitzvah, but for adulthood?

FOOTNOTES
[1] Matt. 28:19,20
[2] John 14:15
[3] John 13:34,35
[4] Psalm 23:1
[5] Numbers 1:3
[6] Ex. 30:14
[7] Phylacteries, miniature boxes containing scriptures worn by Orthodox Jews on the left arm and forehead during prayer.
[8] Deut. 16:16
[9] Luke 2:42
[10] John 1:12; Gal 3:26
[11] John 5:39
[12] 2 Samuel 12:23
[13] Aboth 5: Mishnah 21
[14] Psalm 100:5
[15] Num. 32:23
[16] Galatians 6:8
[17] Luke 16:25-28
[18] James/Jacob 4:4
[19] Joshua 24:15

Chapter Ten

Celebrating Biblical and Jewish Holidays

The Biblical Jewish year is organized according to the Feasts of Israel which God instituted in Leviticus 23. This chapter in Leviticus presents God's yearly schedule which illustrates His redemptive plan, and is His appointment calendar with His redeemed people. As we celebrate the feasts each year, we are incorporating, reinforcing and deepening the Lord's redemptive values into the lives of our families. Of course, if you are attending a messianic congregation, you will be both aware of the yearly calendar of biblical holidays and given opportunity to celebrate them. Each of the feasts has both intrinsic values and prophetic significance as well. In the appendix is a chart showing the feasts and their New Covenant fulfillments (see page 194).

All of the feasts can have an application in the home, and are home oriented, as with Passover. Many messianic congregations will have a congregational Seder, as well as encouraging families to have their own home Seder. To celebrate Passover at home a *Messianic Passover Haggadah* will help you and the family enjoy the celebration of our deliverance from bondage in Egypt and from sin.

There are a total of seven Feasts that can actually be noted in Leviticus 23. Of these seven, three (Passover, Pentecost and Tabernacles) are called *Pilgrim Feasts*, when all Jewish men were required to go to Jeruslem to celebrate the Feast.[1]

PASSOVER WEEK (LEVITICUS 23:5-11)

The picture of redemption begins to unfold in the spring, with the feasts of Passover, Unleavened Bread, and First Fruits. Since the days of Moses and the Exodus, the Jewish people in general, and Messianic believers in particular, continue to celebrate these feasts each year. Tragically, the traditional Jewish community remains unaware of the great truths these feast days point to: *Messiah our Passover* has died for our sins,[2] thereby taking away our sins,[3] and has become *the First Fruits from the dead.*[4] The Passover Seder is a time to celebrate the redemption from bondage in Egypt. This pictures our redemption from sin and judgment through the Lamb of God.

The Feast of Unleavened Bread/Passover is also a challenge for many of us to find new ways to prepare a meal with Matzah. It helps us understand to a degree our people's cry in the wilderness, "Manna again? Oy!" In any case, eating unleavened bread is instructional for the family. Since leaven is a picture of the corruption of sin,[5] we can better understand that in order to celebrate our redemption, we must remove "leaven" from the home—and the heart.

PENTECOST (LEV. 23:15-18)

Fifty days later *Pentecost* (or *Shavuot, Weeks*) caps off the spring feasts. Biblically this is another first fruits harvest feast that is traditionally celebrated as the *season of the giving of the Law*. For believers it further typifies the birth of the Body of Messiah through the giving of *Ruach HaKodesh* (Holy Spirit.) As Yeshua was the First Fruits from the dead at Passover, believers in Him are also called First Fruits through Pentecost. That is, we are First Fruits, new creations alive in Messiah.[6] Pentecost is a great time to study the whole issue of first fruits.

As first fruits were always set apart for God's use only, so our families should be living for the Lord. As *Shavuot* celebrates the first fruits of the wheat harvest,[7] enjoying special foods made from wheat gives us opportunity to consider how we are 'first fruits in Messiah', and very special to Him.

The Feast of Trumpets (Lev. 23:23-25), or Rosh Hashana, The Jewish New Year

Today the *Feast of Trumpets* is commonly called *Rosh Hashana,* or the Jewish New Year. When the Jewish people came out of the Babylonian captivity, they adopted the Babylonian civil New Year as their own. Biblically, and prophetically speaking, the Feast of Trumpets calls our attention to the future sounding of the trumpet of God. At this future event, the Body of Messiah will be gathered to Messiah in what is called *the Rapture*. In your home, this is a great time for the family to discuss what it means to be ready for Messiah's return.[8] Also, Rosh Hashana is a special time to remember our new life in Yeshua.[9]

Yom Kippur, the Day of Atonement (Lev. 23:26-32)

Ten days after Rosh Hashana the "feast" of *Yom Kippur*, the Day of Atonement, is observed. Traditionally, Yom Kippur is a time for Jewish people to 'get right with God' individually, and fasting, rather than feasting is the norm for many Jewish people. Biblically, Yom Kippur is a day for Israel to be restored to God as a nation.[10] It also points to the future day when Israel as a nation will return to Messiah.[11] This is a time for the family to give praise for the atonement we receive by faith in Yeshua. Many Messianic believers observe this day by fasting and praying for our people, Israel, and for the peace of Jerusalem.[12]

The Feast of Sukkot, Booths or Tabernacles (Lev. 23:33-43)

Finally comes the feast of *Sukkot* (*Booths or Tabernacles*), which is also called the *Feast of Ingathering*.[13] Today it is celebrated as a final harvest festival, and it is accompanied with great joy for the provision of God for His people. It will one day, however, mark the final harvest and gathering together of all people to the Lord as King, and will be celebrated with the most joyous celebration of all time![14] Today you can celebrate Sukkot by building a sukkah, (as in picture on page 136), in your yard. Or as Miriam and I used to do in Yonkers, NY, build one on your 3rd floor terrace! Building a booth provides a hands on opportunity to celebrate Messiah's provision, leadership and security in our lives. It also serves as a public testimony to both your family and your community of your faith in the Lord. This booth pictures Messiah's protection and provision for our lives.[15]

Two other festivals: Purim and Hanukkah

There are two feasts celebrated by our people today that do not appear in the Leviticus 23 passage. These are *Purim* and *Hanukkah*, which occured much later in history, and are very relevant to our faith in Messiah. Purim, which was established in Esther's day, reminds us that despite anti-Semitism, God's promise to keep us as a people is the very hope of Israel. Purim is celebrated by publicly reading the book of Esther, often re-enacted as a play.

Hanukkah celebrates the rededication of the Temple in 165 B.C. in Jerusalem. After the temple had been desecrated by the Syrian invaders, the Maccabee family led the Jewish revolt, recapturing, cleansing, and rededicating the temple for holy worship. This holiday is mentioned only in John 10:22,23, where Messiah celebrated Hanukkah in Jerusalem. In truth, Messiah is the greater Maccabee who in His death rededicated the present spiritual Temple of God—all believers in Him.[16]

Today Hanukkah is an eight-day festival, and is celebrated with the lighting of the *hanukkiah*, which is a nine-candle menorah. As we light the candles during this time, we remember the light of the menorah in the Temple, which pictures Messiah. He is the light of Israel, and the light of the world! Hanukkah also reminds us that as God used the Maccabees to rededicate the Temple, our bodies are the temple of the Ruach HaKodesh, and we need to rededicate ourselves to the Lord.[17] For only a dedicated Temple is blessed by God.

I have only touched on each of the feasts in this chapter. There is a wealth of rich, wonderful teaching found in the feasts that can actually impact your life and the lives of those around you. For further study, see WMM's book *"The Feasts of Israel"*, where you'll discover profound, even prophetic revelations of God's purpose in Messiah that are illustrated through the feasts!

Questions
For your further study and consideration

As a believer in Messiah, what significance do you find between the Levitical feasts and Yeshua the Messiah?

How do the feasts further demonstrate the validity of Yeshua's claims as Messiah? Please explain.

How you plan to observe any of the feasts in the coming year? With your congregation? In your home?

Footnotes
[1] Deut 16:16
[2] 1 Cor. 5:7
[3] John 1:29
[4] 1 Cor. 15:20,23
[5] Lev. 2:11, 1 Cor. 5:8
[6] James/Jacob 1:17,18
[7] Exodus 34:22
[8] see 1 John 2:28; 1 Thess. 4:13-18; 1 Cor. 15:51,52
[9] Romans 6:4-6
[10] Lev.16; also Lev. 23:26-32
[11] Zech. 12:10-13:1; Romans 11:25-27
[12] Psalm 122:6; Romans 10:1
[13] Exodus. 23:16
[14] see Zechariah 14:16-19; John 7:2, 37-39
[15] see Revelation 7:15
[16] 1 Cor. 6:18-20
[17] 1 Cor. 6:19

For more information on *"The Feasts of Israel"*, *"The Messianic Passover Haggadah"*, *and other Messianic resources,* see page 198.

Chapter Eleven

Celebrating The "Christian" Holidays

The phrase "Christian holidays" generally refers to Christmas and Easter. Though quite popular and observed by millions around the world, neither of these are recorded in the Bible as a holiday, nor is there any biblical mandate for their celebration by believers. Unfortunately it has become such a normative part of 'Christianity' that it can seem unnatural for a Christian, or Believer in Yeshua, to not celebrate or acknowledge these two events in some fashion. All Messianic believers are certainly to be thankful that Messiah was born, and that He was resurrected. Whether or not Messiah was born on December 25th, and whether or not there were bunnies and eggs at the Resurrection, are different questions altogether. In any case, should you choose to celebrate the birth and resurrection of Messiah, there needs to be biblical reference for there to be any practical relevance.

CHRISTMAS

The celebration of Christmas began in the year A.D. 98, but it was forty years later before it was officially adopted as a religious festival. It wasn't until about the fifth century A.D. that the day of its celebration became permanently fixed on the 25th day of December. Up until then it had been observed at various times of the year—in December, in April, and in May, but most frequently in January. Though its popularity grew through the centuries, not all believers chose to participate in Christmas. In fact, some very pious Christians did not think it was biblical, nor was it a spiritual issue for them. The Pilgrims of Thanksgiving Day fame condemned all church festivals, and spent their first Christmas in America working hard the entire day amid cold and stormy weather.

But times change, and it is customary in many countries to celebrate Christmas. When our sons were young they wanted what they saw the neighborhood non-Jewish kids had—a Christmas tree. Oy. What was I to do? I sought a way to redeem this holiday and edify my family in a Jewish frame of reference. I explained to my sons how a Christmas tree wasn't our custom, but we would have our own celebration—a birthday party for Yeshua! Praise the Lord, there just happened to be a Carvel ice cream store right down the street. So each year we would get an ice cream cake and decorate it with "Happy Birthday, Messiah Yeshua!" written with icing. Our kids were quite happy, and as we ate it, we talked about the biblical account of Messiah's birth, and my boys began to understand the religious issues that challenge Messianic believers at this season.

Of course it was important as well to be a witness to my unsaved family. Amazingly, though we maintained a Jewish home, every year they assumed that *this year* I would get a Christmas tree. It was hard for them to understand that faith in Messiah did not make me a Gentile. But on the other hand, because I maintained a Jewish testimony with fervent faith in Yeshua, they saw that I was committed to live as a Jew. More importantly, it's vital to honor the Lord in all we do. He needs to be the center of all our celebrations, *"for whatever you do in word or deed, do it all in the name of the Lord Yeshua."*[1]

Santa Claus

Regarding the Santa Claus tradition, we must be careful not to mislead our children. Santa Claus, as it is spun each year—flying reindeer, Santa coming down the chimney, etc.—make for a sweet story, but it simply isn't true. In fact, it is a substitute for the fact of Messiah's incarnation and His miraculous entrance into this world through the virgin birth.

Our children need to understand the difference between biblical fact and worldly fiction, between spiritual reality and foolish fantasy. These are not harmless issues. If you mislead and "fib" to your children about the truth in this one area, how will your child know if you're telling the truth about Yeshua in other areas? In reality, Santa and other such ideas are simply terrible substitutes for and distractions from the truth of Messiah.

REDEEM THE TIME, RECOVER THE GIFT

Though we live in a confused, materialistic, Santa-saturated world, we can still be a light shining in the darkness, a star of Bethlehem, if you will. We have the opportunity to emphasize the reality of Messiah's birth, and what His coming means for each of us, and for all people.

Now for the sake of your family, particularly if you are Jewish, it's important for them to see Christmas from a Jewish viewpoint—through Jewish eyes. It's ordinarily difficult, if not impossible, for most Jewish people to understand the reality of Messiah's birth in the typical Christmas celebration. For instance, the emphasis at Christmas on 'buying gifts', the push for holiday sales, etc. Contrast that with *Emmanuel*—a tiny Jewish baby born to a poor Jewish couple in a humble stable in Israel. *Why* He came is all but a mystery to our pleasure-mad world, and sadly, even to some who would claim to belong to Him. Why did Messiah come? Yeshua said, *"The Son of man came not to be served, but to serve, and to give his life a ransom for many."*[2]

That Messiah is the "Reason for the Season" simply doesn't compute in the way the holiday is commonly portrayed. There's just too much 'Gentile wrapping paper' covering the Jewish gift of God, Yeshua. To clearly see the truth of His birth, we need to see it through Jewish eyes—the eyes of Micah, Isaiah, Matthew and Paul. Here are some Scriptural perspectives on Messiah's birth.

THE BIRTH PLACE OF MESSIAH WAS TO BE BETHLEHEM, ISRAEL

It was prophesied in Micah 5:2...

> *But as for you, Bethlehem Ephratah, too little to be among the clans of Judah, from you One will go forth for Me to be ruler in Israel. His goings forth are from long ago, from the days of eternity.*

Most believers in Yeshua are aware of this Messianic prophecy and its fulfillment as recorded in Matthew and Luke:

> *Now after Jesus was born in Bethlehem of Judea in the days of Herod the king* (Matthew 2:1); *Joseph also went up from Galilee, from the city of Nazareth, to Judea, to the city of David which is called Bethlehem, because he was of the house and family of David, in order to register along with Mary, who was engaged to him, and was with child* (Luke 2:4,5).

But what some may not realize is that even before Yeshua came, the rabbis recognized the Micah 5:2 portion as referring to Messiah. In the *Targums* (the rabbinic paraphrases written c. 100 B.C. which the rabbis used to teach the common people), we see written:

> And you, O Bethlehem Ephrath, you who were too small to be numbered among the thousands of the house of Judah, from you shall come forth before Me

the Messiah, to exercise dominion over Israel, he whose name was mentioned from before, from the days of creation (Targum on Micah 5:1).

Thus, we see the name "Messiah" is identified also by the rabbis with this prophecy from Micah. So when certain people say that the birth of Messiah in Tanakh (the Old Covenant) is nonsense and *goyisha* (Gentile) we can say, "not at all, even the rabbis recognized Messiah's birth from the Prophet Micah!"

MESSIAH IS APPROACHABLE

But the most wonderful part of this prophecy is that the Scriptures teach of the innate humility of the Messiah. Can you imagine the God of the universe coming in the flesh as a humble servant? If that was not humbling enough, He chooses to be born in the backwater province of the Roman Empire, Judea, in the tiny town of Bethlehem. But His greatest humility is that He would humble Himself to death on the cross. Through Jewish eyes we see that Messiah was demonstrating the humility of a God who loves us more than His own glorious position as God. This quality of humility is what the New Covenant consistently presents in Yeshua:

Come to Me, all who are weary and heavy-laden, and I will give you rest. Take My yoke upon you and learn from Me, for I am gentle and humble in heart, and you will find rest for your souls (Matthew 11:28,29).

Have this attitude in yourselves which was also in Messiah Yeshua, who, although He existed in the form of God, did not regard equality with God a thing to be grasped, but emptied Himself, taking the form of a bond-servant, and being made in the likeness of men. Being found in appearance as a man, He humbled

Himself by becoming obedient to the point of death, even death on a cross (Philippians 2:5-8).

What a wonderful oppotiunity to encourage the family in the godly characteristic of humilty.

THE GOOD NEWS OF EMMANUEL

In the book of Isaiah, chapters 7-11 are commonly called "the Good News of Emmanuel." It is actually God's birth announcement of Messiah—sent seven hundred years in advance!

Messiah was to be born of a virgin according to Isaiah 7:14...

Therefore the Lord Himself will give you a sign: Behold, a virgin will be with child and bear a son, and she will call His name Immanuel.

God would a have unique entrance for the unique One, the Messiah. Those who deny the virgin birth must also deny the reality of miracles, the fact of God and the very existence of the Jewish people! If one accepts any true miracle as a supernatural work, then why should this one make a difference? If there truly is a God at all, then the Creator of all should have no problem with a virgin birth. Let us not forget that the Jewish people got their start through a miracle birth or two, via Sarah, Rebecca and Rachel.[3] In the first two chapters of Matthew and Luke, the New Covenant records the fulfillment of this prophesied miracle. But the true miracle of God continues. In Messiah Yeshua, every one who believes in Him experiences a "miracle birth," and becomes a child of God.

Messiah was actually prophesied to be God incarnate. In Isaiah 7:14 Messiah is called *Emmanuel,* which means "God is with us." Isaiah also says—

> *For unto us a child will be born, unto us a son will be given; And the government will rest on His shoulders; And His name will be called Wonderful Counselor,* **Mighty God***, Eternal Father, Prince of Peace*
> (Isaiah 9:6).
> *A remnant will return, the remnant of Jacob, to* **the Mighty God** (Isaiah 10:21).

The birth itself was a double miracle:
1) A virgin giving birth to a child divinely conceived; and...
2) the child Himself being God incarnate, the divine Son of God.[4]

That God is able to come in the flesh speaks of His omnipotence. That God would want to come in the flesh speaks of His love. It's no surprise that most Jewish people do not believe in Yeshua, since Isaiah prophesied that only 'a remnant of Jacob would return.' So, the New Covenant reveals the fulfillment that *"there has also come to be at the present time a remnant according to God's gracious choice."*[5]

HE WAS TO BE OF THE DAVIDIC LINE

Several portions of Scripture speak of Messiah being not only the *righteous* King, but also the rightful King.

> ✿ *Then he said, "Listen now, O house of David! Is it too slight a thing for you to try the patience of men, that you will try the patience of my God as well?*(Isa. 7:13).
> ✿ *On the throne of David and over his kingdom*(Isa. 9:7).
> ✿ *Then a shoot will spring from the stem of Jesse, And a branch from his roots will bear fruit* (Isaiah 11:1).

✿ *"Behold, the days are coming," declares the LORD, "When I will raise up for David a righteous Branch; and He will reign as king and act wisely And do justice and righteousness in the land. "In His days Judah will be saved, and Israel will dwell securely; and this is His name by which He will be called, 'The LORD our righteousness'"* (Jeremiah 23:5,6).

God assured the House of David that it would continue forever through a miraculous virgin birth occuring in David's family line. As the *Son of David*, Messiah would be the One authorized to rule and thus have the authority to rule. As *Mighty God*, we give Him our worship in prayer. As *King* we give Him our obedience in practice. He is Whom the New Covenant declares:

You shall name Him Yeshua. He will be great and will be called the Son of the Most High; and the Lord God will give Him the throne of His father David; and He will reign over the house of Jacob forever, and His kingdom will have no end (Luke 1:31-33).

HE WAS TO HAVE THE FULLNESS OF THE SPIRIT

The Spirit of the LORD will rest on Him, the spirit of wisdom and understanding, the spirit of counsel and strength, the spirit of knowledge and the fear of the LORD. And He will delight in the fear of the LORD, and He will not judge by what His eyes see, nor make a decision by what His ears hear (Isaiah 11:2,3).

These seven-fold qualities of the Spirit of God are the "seven eyes" of the Lamb in Revelation 5:6. This anointing[6] spoken of is what makes Him the Messiah, the Anointed One, and the Appointed One—appointed by God to bring salvation. As Son of David He has the spiritual power to judge authoritatively, as the Anointed One He has the spiritual perception to judge righteously.

He was to be sought by Gentiles as well

Then in that day the nations will resort to the root of Jesse, Who will stand as a signal for the peoples; and His resting place will be glorious (Isaiah 11:10).

One of the evidences of the true Jewish Messiah is that *Gentiles* will believe in Him. Though He might not be Mr. Popularity, He would be able to meet the needs of all people. It's no wonder that right after His birth Magi from the East came to *honor Him who was born King of the Jews.*[7] But why would Gentiles find him attractive? By faith in Messiah, Gentile believers receive salvation along with Jewish believers. This is a further miracle of God—believing Gentiles would be made fellow heirs and spiritual family with believing Jews! The New Covenant describes the fulfillment of this hope in Ephesians 2:14-16.

For [Yeshua] Himself is our peace, who made both groups into one and broke down the barrier of the dividing wall, by abolishing in His flesh the enmity, which is the Law of commandments contained in ordinances, so that in Himself He might make the two [Jew and Gentile] into one new man, thus establishing peace, and might reconcile them both in one body to God through the cross, by it having put to death the enmity.

Through Jewish eyes we see the birth of the greater Son of David, the Mighty God, the Messiah, the Savior of Jew and Gentile alike. No reindeer, no holly wreaths, no Santa Claus, no commercialism. Only the truth of God's humble, yet glorious love gift to all who will believe. For a truly happy holiday, celebrate the new life found in Yeshua!

What About Easter?

Regarding the celebration of Messiah's resurrection, it is only in light of Passover that we celebrate 'Resurrection Sunday' and can appreciate the deeper meaning of this glorious event. So why is it called *Easter*, and what does it mean for the believer?

The name *Easter*, as it's called in the West, comes from ancient pagan origins, namely the Babylonian fertility goddess, *Ishtar*. She was worshiped in various forms and under various names: *Astarte* of the Canaanites, etc.; *Diana*, of the Ephesians[8]; *Venus*, from the Roman pantheon; or as the Saxons called her *Eostre*. Each year about the time of Passover, sacrifices were offered to Ishtar in celebration of the Spring solstice. This included shameful 'worship' practices, which involved temple prostitution, and the like. The worship of Ishtar as the goddess of fertility, led to the traditions of rabbits, the Easter Bunny, and painting and hiding eggs. Once again, we can see activities which at best distract our attention away from the Lord and the great redemption He has accomplished for us. The wonder and awe little children feel when considering a magical Santa Claus or Peter Cottontail (both of whom win our children's affection by giving gifts) is but a poor substitute for knowing and loving God. Because children are so impressionable and easily convinced by adults, we cannot afford to be ignorant on these issues.[9]

What we are sowing into their hearts and minds now will play a large part in directing their lives in the future. In addition to distracting from the resurrection, there is the potential for combining pagan ritual with Biblical truth, which has always proven to be a deadly mixture. As Messiah said, *"the hour cometh, and now is, when the true worshippers shall worship the Father in spirit and in truth: for the Father seeketh such to worship him."*[10]

HE IS RISEN. THAT'S THE TRUTH!

It is important to tell the truth to your children about the resurrection of Yeshua. The fact is, Messiah rose from the dead, and His resurrection is the foundation of the entire Messianic faith. Messiah, as the Lamb of God, was slain on Passover, and as the Firstfruits of the Resurrection, He was raised on the Feast of Firstfruits.[11] Why? His resurrection was verification that God was pleased with, and approved of His atonement for our sins, and raised Him back to life to validate it!

Messiah lives today, and He is real. The Easter bunny isn't. Though we have liberty, our celebration should be careful not to include strange and originally pagan trappings. This can actually take away from honoring our Lord. When He returns, Messiah isn't coming 'hopping down the bunny trail.' He is coming in the clouds, and we look forward to meeting Him when He comes again![12] Therefore, let us rejoice in the fact that He is risen, and lives forever!

QUESTIONS
FOR YOUR FURTHER STUDY AND CONSIDERATION

Now that you understand the background of the Christmas and Easter, how do they affect your life as a Messianic believer? If your spouse isn't Jewish, how does this effect his or her life as a Gentile believer?

Regarding the Christian Holidays, do you believe they provide an opportunity to present the Good News of Messiah, or would you rather avoid them altogether? Can you modify them in order to provide a witness for Yeshua?

How do you plan to approach the issues regarding Christmas(The birth of Messiah) and Easter(The resurrection of Messiah) with your children?

FOOTNOTES

[1] Colossians 3:17
[2] Mt. 20:28; also John 18:37
[3] Gen. 18:14; 25:21; 30:22
[4] see Luke 1:35
[5] Romans 11:5
[6] see Psalm 45:6-8
[7] Matthew 2:1-12
[8] see Acts 19:24-35
[9] see 2 Corinthians 2:11
[10] John 4:23
[11] Leviticus 23:10,11; see 1 Corinthians 15:21-23
[12] 1 Corinthians 15:51-53; 1 Thes. 4:16-18

Chapter Twelve

Your Testimony at Home

> And these words,
> which I am commanding you today,
> shall be on your heart; and you shall
> teach them diligently to your sons...
> — Moses
> Deuteronomy 6:6,7a

> Fathers, do not exasperate your children;
> instead, bring them up in the training
> and instruction of the Lord.
> — Rabbi Shaul (Paul)
> Ephesians 6:4

Your testimony is generally a "home front" issue. The fact that you go to a Messianic congregation will not impress people as much as having Messianic values at home. This is especially true for your own children.

Your Messianic lifestyle speaks of the Jewishness of your faith, and celebrating the holidays and Shabbat at home is often a more important testimony than what you merely say. For instance, lighting the candles on Shabbat and pronouncing the blessings, or *Brachot,* over the bread and cup is a wonderful tradition, and an opportunity to instruct the family about the "Sabbath rest" we have in Messiah Yeshua.[1] After all, He is *the light of the world, the bread of life,* and *the true vine!* In the appendix are blessings for celebrating a Shabbat meal at home.[2]

TEACHING YOUR CHILDREN AT HOME

Your most important ministry from the Lord is to your family. Concerning children, it is your privilege and responsibility to *"train up a child in the way he is to go."*[3] No one cares more about your child's spiritual development than the Lord does. In Deuteronomy 6:6,7 He commands—

> *These words that I give you today are to be upon your hearts. You shall teach them diligently to your children, and shall talk of them when you sit in your house, when you walk by the way, when you lie down, and when you rise up.*

WHAT ARE WE TO TEACH?

In verse 6 the word "them" (*you shall talk of them*) refers to <u>these words</u> which are to be *upon your heart*. These are the words we teach: Who the Lord is—(6:4) *Hear, O Israel: The LORD our God, the LORD is One*; and our love for Him— (6:5) *You shall love the LORD your God with all your heart and all your soul and all your might*— (6:7) *to your children*. Thus we are to teach of the nature of God, and a wholehearted response to His nature. Because He *is* God, He *cannot lie*[4]; therefore we are to *walk in the truth.*[5] In so doing, as an expression of our love for the Lord, we become people of integrity. He is the Truth, and will always lead us in the truth.

WHO ARE WE TO TEACH?

The Hebrew word for children (*b'nai*) in Deuteronomy 6:7 is used elsewhere in the Scriptures referring to *disciples—sons of the prophets.*[6] This verse not only applies to your personal discipleship issues, but also to raising your natural children in *the reverance and admonition of the Lord.*[7] Our own children should be our 'number one' disciples. Take a personal interest in teaching and praying for them. As they grow, you will spiritually grow with them as you minister to them in grace and in the word of God.

Remember, to have 'wise children' there are two primary needs: to love your children *unconditionally*, and to give *consistent* discipline. Think of a home where there's a lot of love, but no discipline: what would the child be like? Yes, a prima donna—thinking the world revolves around her or him. Now think of a home where there is heavy discipline but no love, what would the home be like? Like a boot camp. What would the child be like who was raised in that environment? Probably stressed out, rigid, constantly seeking approval based on their performance. Now imagine a home with neither love nor discipline? What would the child be like? This is the classic sociopath—unconcerned for others and lacking the self-discipline to restrain their own lusts.

But in a home where there is *both unconditional love* and *consistent discipline,* we find children who have the wisdom to be concerned for the needs of others, yet also have the discipline to restrain their own desires in obedience to the Lord.

HOW ARE WE TO TEACH?
Notice carefully what the Scripture text says:

1. **PERSONALLY:** *"You shall teach them."*

Sending our kids to Shabbat School (or in some cases Sunday School) is no substitute for teaching God's truth to our own kids at home. Though your children should be taught at Shabbat School, this does not replace your responsibility to *train up your child in the way he is to go.*[8]

Along with giving thanks for your meals, start having a family devotion time right away. Teaching our kids at home involves reading the Bible to them, even when they are little. Sometimes a children's Bible on their level will be quite helpful.

As they get older, read them stories from daily devotionals, or perhaps share a personal insight from your own Bible study with them at meal time. A lengthy, theological discourse isn't necessary, just consistently share from your heart simple truths from God's Word. Then Shabbat School will hopefully complement and reinforce the values your child is learning at home. You'll be amazed at how meaningful this time will become, and rejoice that through your life the truth of God is passing from generation to generation.

2. **PRACTICALLY:** *"...and shall talk of them when you sit in your house, when you walk by the way, when you lie down, and when you rise up."*[9]

If His words are upon our hearts, talking about Him becomes an everyday, ordinary occurrence. We demonstrate how God's Word permeates our lives whether we realize it or not—as we shop, as we are at work, or at play. God's Word is the key to successful living in this world.[10] As you discipline yourself to apply God's Word in your own life, you will be able to teach your children as well.

One additional thought: whether your kids go to public or private school, or are home-schooled, stay involved in their lives. Become acquainted with all of the adults who are their teachers—and know what they are teaching. You have the responsiblilty, and the right, to know.

3. **PERSUASIVELY:** *"...teach them diligently."*

Diligently in the Hebrew is the word *shinon*. The word *shinon* means *sharp* or *pierce,* as *a sharp sword* or *piercing arrow.*[11] The emphasis is on teaching God's Word in such a way that the truth pierces their hearts and impacts their lives.

This occurs only when God's word has the pre-eminence in your life—the truth must first be upon *your* heart. To the degree God's Word is upon your heart—*personally*—and permeates your everyday life—*practically*—is the degree to which it impacts the lives of your kids as well—*persuasively*. May Yeshua bless you and your family in and through His Word.

QUESTIONS
FOR YOUR FURTHER STUDY AND CONSIDERATION

What customs do you observe in your home that are consistant with a Messianic lifestyle?

Do you believe that it is important to perpetuate the Jewish community and culture, particularly in a Messianic/Biblical context? Why or why not?

How are you incorporating a regular devotional/teaching time with your children in keeping with Deuteronomy 6:4-9?

FOOTNOTES
[1] Hebrews 4
[2] For more on the blessings, see *"Blessings in Hebrew CD"* on page 198, or contact *Word of Messiah Ministries*.
[3] Proverbs 22:6
[4] Titus 1:2
[5] 3 John 1:4
[6] 2 Kings 2:7,15
[7] Ephesians 6:1
[8] Proverbs 22:6
[9] Deut. 6:7
[10] Psalm 1:2,3; Joshua 1:7,8
[11] Psalm 45:5

Chapter Thirteen

Dealing with Death in the Family

It is better to go to a house of mourning than to go to a house of feasting, because that is the end of every man, and the living will take it to heart.
— Solomon
Ecclesiastes 7:2

I am the resurrection and the life; he who believes in Me shall live even if he dies, and everyone who lives and believes in Me shall never die.
— Yeshua
John 11:26

For most Jewish believers, a death in the family is a severely traumatic event. Most times the Jewish believer has few fellow family members that have yet come to faith in Messiah. The Bible declares that without personal faith in Messiah Yeshua there is no salvation.[1] Tragically, what this means is that these unsaved family members who die without Messiah are eternally separated from God, and will be judged for their sins.[2]

WHAT IS DEATH?

In the Scriptures death is defined, not as cessation of existence, but as separation—from the body (natural death) and from God (permanent, spiritual, or the *second death*[3]). Contrary to popular opinion, at death we don't get 'recycled' (reincarnation), nor do we cease to exist (annihilation). The Scriptures declare without ambiguity, *"it is appointed for a man once to die, and after that the judgment."* [4]

IS THAT FAIR?

How are we to deal with this matter? Since we are assured that *"the judge of all the earth will do right,"*[5] we know that even eternal separation from God is what is "right" for our unsaved relatives who are departed. The truth is we all deserve hell and judgment for our sins, but Yeshua took our place and paid for our sins. In fact, anyone who will trust in Messiah will *not* get what they *do deserve*—righteous judgment; and *will* get what they *don't deserve*—forgiveness and grace, mercy and salvation.[6]

IN DEATH, GOD IS MERCIFUL

In Isaiah 57:1 we read,

> *The righteous man perishes, and no man takes it to heart; And devout men are taken away, while no one understands. For the righteous man is taken away from evil.*

Taken away from evil? Yes, God knows what is up ahead for each of us. In His wisdom and mercy, God sometimes takes a person through death to avoid an even worse situation that would occur in their future. As hard as it may be to understand, there are worse things than death. A debilitating and traumatic illness can sometimes bring years of humiliation and financial catastrophe for the surviving family. For others, like King Hezekiah, when he prayed regarding his impending death, God granted him fifteen additional years. Unfortunately it led to the spiritual low point of his life, and he ended up ruining the stability of the nation, and the future for his children and his people Israel.[7] For Hezekiah, and our people, it seems it would have been better if God had not answered his prayer and taken him sooner. For those who will not accept Messiah, it is better that the Lord take them sooner, lest they add additional sin to their judgment.[8]

Though this is a difficult subject, in all things we can trust that the *"Judge of all the earth will do right."* We know that no one loves our family members more than God, and no one cares for their loss more than the He, Who gave Himself for lost sinners.[9]

Ministering to Those who Mourn

The Scriptures teach us to *"weep with those who weep."*[10] This very compassion is demonstrated by Messiah at the funeral of Lazarus. Though Yeshua knew that He was about to raise him from the dead, He still identified with those who were in sorrow over Lazarus' death. Just as Isaiah tells us *"in all their affliction, He was afflicted,"*[11] we see God's compassion manifested in Yeshua's response to the grief of others—*"Yeshua wept."*[12] Messiah's love should be seen in those who follow Him.

MINISTERING TO A BELIEVER

When visiting a believer who has lost a *believing* loved one, remember with all loss there is pain, but in Messiah there is a sure hope. In this situation we are reminded—

> *But we do not want you to be uninformed, brethren, about those who are asleep, so that you will not grieve as do the rest who have no hope. For God has not destined us for wrath, but for obtaining salvation through our Lord Messiah Yeshua* (1 Thessalonians 4:13; 5:9).

We should certainly expect a believer to mourn the loss of a believing loved one, but that mourning is not out of despair, it's out of love. The truth is that one day there will be a wonderful reunion. In this case let us focus on the faith of the one who has "graduated" and the certainty that *to be absent from the body is to be at home with the Lord.*[13] The loved one who is separated by death from our presence is now "*at home*" rejoicing in the presence of the Lord!

When visiting a believer who has lost a *nonbelieving* loved one, we find a very painful situation. In fact, the more mature the believer is, the more painful their sense of loss may be. The believer may be acutely aware that the state of their loved one is eternal separation, not only from themselves, but from God.

As far as I know, when my father died, he died without the Lord. It was unbearably painful for me. There were some well meaning, but false-comforters, who shared what were meant to be encouraging words—"I'm sure the Lord will save your father because of your faith." No, I knew better; each person must believe for himself. Another said, "I'm sure your father will get a second chance." As much as it hurts to realize it, I know that there is no second chance after death. But, there was some counsel that did help. I came to understand that no one loved my father more than the Lord. God shared my pain. This reality helped me to find comfort and fellowship with God in my misery. Beyond my pain and my own understanding, I could trust in the Lord's righteousness which even my father himself would now admit is just and fair.

Also, regarding my father's lost spiritual state, I previously used the phrase "as far as I know." It's not that God's Word is unclear, but we don't know what transpired in my father's heart during his last moments before he died. It is possible that though he was unable to communicate *to me*, he was still able in his heart to trust in the Lord and be saved. Perhaps in those last moments my many years of witnessing to him came to his mind, and in his soul he cried out, "Yeshua, save me!" Knowing God's mercy, this thought is some comfort for my aching heart. So when visiting with believers who have lost a loved one who never confessed the Lord, these are some things to keep in mind and share.

MINISTERING TO A NON-BELIEVER

Visiting a non-believer who has lost a *non-believing* loved one is unfortunately the normal Jewish scenario. In this situation, it is important not to give false comfort—such as, "I'm sure he's in a better place"—but to give true comfort. Your quiet prayerful presence is a comfort. You may consider saying, "I'll be praying for you," and "let me know if I can be of any help." However, many times words may seem meaningless to the one who is grieving. Sometimes just being there with the mourner is a comfort. Generally, this is not the time, nor the place for a theological chit-chat on the afterlife: so don't be drawn into such discussions. Rather, remember especially at such times these words, *"Conduct yourselves with wisdom toward outsiders, making the most of the opportunity. Let your speech always be with grace..."*[14]

When visiting a non-believer who has lost a *believing* loved one, you may want to share the truths from our first scenario, but be very careful. A non-believer in Messiah may not even believe in God, or they may be angry at God and not open at this time to the truth of the Scriptures. So go slowly, with a quiet attitude, yet with hopefulness. In this case you can, simply and quietly, assure them that the loved one who died is in a better place, and that their pain is over forever. But as noted, be very sensitive, for these words may not be accepted.

Your *relationship* with the mourner, and not necessarily with the deceased, will make a great deal of difference on how much you can share.

In all these situations be in prayer. *Ruach HaKodesh* will guide and direct you, and give you a ministry of comfort to the one who mourns. In so doing, you will be Messiah's instrument of grace, and represent God, Who is *"the Father of Mercies and God of all Comfort."*[15]

SHOULD BELIEVERS 'SIT SHIVAH' AND SAY 'THE KADDISH'?

Since *sitting Shivah* (Heb. *quietness*) is a period of mourning, generally for seven days, there is great value in this. It is an opportunity for you to mourn the passing of the loved one, and to seek the Lord in prayer and study His word. This will be a great comfort to you.[16] While sitting Shivah with my father following the death of my mother, I had an unusual opportunity to comfort my dad. I read to him from the Psalms, then the Prophets. Then I began to read from John 11, regarding the death and resurrection of Lazarus:

> *Yeshua said to her, "I am the resurrection and the life; he who believes in Me will live even if he dies, and everyone who lives and believes in Me will never die. Do you believe this?" She said to Him, "Yes, Lord; I have believed that You are the Messiah, the Son of God, even He who comes into the world." When she had said this, she went away and called Mary her sister, saying secretly, "The Teacher is here and is calling for you." And when she heard it, she got up quickly and was coming to Him* (John 11:25-29).

When my father heard the words *"she got up quickly"* he declared, "She got up from sitting Shivah? —but that's only for Messiah? Aha, she considered Him the Messiah!" So, you never know what comfort and witness the Lord may give during Shivah.

IN DEATH I WILL PRAISE THEE

Kaddish, which means *holy*, is a traditional prayer that is said from the day of burial, daily for the first eleven months, and on the anniversary of the death. Interestingly, this prayer never mentions the dead, but continually praises God, which is certainly an appropriate perspective. Though it can be difficult when sorrowing over departed loved ones, developing an attitude of thanksgiving and praise is key for coping with this most difficult of human experiences. The Kaddish is traditionally only read, sung or recited when there is a *minyan*,[17] but it is a lovely and comforting meditation, and helps us appreciate God's soveriegnty and care for us in all things. The Kaddish is found on the following page.

Kaddish in English

*May the great Name of God be exalted
and sanctified, throughout the world,
which He has created according to His will.*

*May His Kingship be established in your lifetime
and in your days, and in the lifetime
of the entire household of Israel,
swiftly and in the near future; and say,
Amen.*

*May His great Name be blessed,
forever and ever.
Blessed, praised, glorified, exalted, extolled,
honored elevated and lauded
be The Name of the Holy One,
Blessed is He—above and beyond
any blessings and hymns,
praises and consolations
which are uttered in the world; and say
Amen.*

*May there be abundant peace from Heaven,
and life, upon us and upon all Israel; and say,
Amen.*

*He who makes peace in His high holy places,
may He bring peace upon us,
and upon all Israel; and say,
Amen.*

KADDISH IN HEBREW
(TRANSLITERATION)

*Yit'ga'dal v'yitkadash sh'meh raba, b'alma di
b'ra chir'uteh v'yamlich mal'chuteh,
b'khai 'yei'chon uv'yomei'chon uv'khai'yei
d'chol beit Yisrael.
Ba'agala uviz'man qariv;
v'imru Amein.*

*Y'hei sh'meh raba m'varach l'alam
ul'almei almaiya.
Yit'barach v'yish'tabach v'yitpa'ar v'yit'
romam v'yit'nasei, v'yithadar v'yit'aleh v'yit'
halal, sh'meh d'qud'sha, b'rich hu l'ela min cal
bir'chata v'shir'ata, tush'b'khata v'nekhe'mata,
da'amiran b'alma;
v'imru Amein.*

*Y'hei sh'lama raba min sh'maiya,
v'khai'yim aleinu v'al kal Yisrael;
v'imru Amein.*

*Oseh shalom bim'romav,
hu ya'aseh shalom aleinu,
v'al cal yisrael;
vimru Amein.*

Questions
For Your Further Study and Consideration

Understanding the love and character of God in Messiah, how can you minister to those who grieve over lost loved ones?

In light of eternity and your own mortality, are there adjustments to your priorities and daily lifestyle that you need to make?

Since there is no second chance after death, how can you plan to share the Good News with the people in your life who don't yet know Messiah?

Footnotes
[1] Isaiah 45:22; Acts 4:12; Deut. 18:18,19
[2] John 3:36, 8:24
[3] Revelation 20:13-15
[4] Hebrews 9:27, see also Daniel 12:2
[5] see Genesis 18:25
[6] For more on the issues of Hell and the fairness of judgment see chapter from *The Messianic Answer Book*
[7] see Isa. 39:1-8
[8] Romans 2:5
[9] John 3:16
[10] Romans 12:15
[11] Isaiah 63:9
[12] John 11:33-35
[13] 2 Corinthians 5:8
[14] Colossians 4:5,6
[15] 2 Cor. 1:3
[16] 2 Corinthians 1:3
[17] A *minyan* is a quorum of 10 Jewish men who are over the age of thirteen.

Chapter Fourteen

Your Faith
and
Your Finances

HE WHO IS FAITHFUL IN WHAT IS LEAST
IS FAITHFUL ALSO IN MUCH;
AND HE WHO IS UNJUST IN WHAT IS LEAST
IS UNJUST ALSO IN MUCH. — YESHUA
LUKE 16:10

GIVE, AND IT WILL BE GIVEN TO YOU;
GOOD MEASURE, PRESSED DOWN,
SHAKEN TOGETHER, RUNNING OVER,
THEY WILL POUR INTO YOUR LAP.
FOR BY YOUR STANDARD OF MEASURE
IT WILL BE MEASURED TO YOU IN RETURN.
— YESHUA
LUKE 6:38

THE RICH RULES OVER THE POOR,
AND THE BORROWER IS SERVANT
TO THE LENDER. — SOLOMON
PROVERBS 22:7

In the area of finances it's often said, "The problem with money is, it doesn't come with instructions!" Well, that's not really true. Though the Scriptures are not merely a "money guide," the Bible does give us quite a bit of expert advise on our finances. No, it's not a way to get rich quick, but rather that we might have God's perspective and wisdom in using our finances. Whether it be our time, talent, or our treasures, the ultimate goal in this and all other matters is that we would honor the Lord in handling our resources. Remember, you're only the manager of the funds, but God is the owner of all things.[1] We're therefore responsible to spend the money entrusted to us in a way that will please Him and reflect His will and character.

Even though the principles apply to all believers, the reasonable, practical wisdom found in the Scriptures will benefit even the unbeliever, when applied.[2]

Your Work Ethic

There is some general wisdom gained from the Scriptures on this subject. Many new believers, or those poorly discipled, do not realize that hard work and practical wisdom are biblical norms for all believers. So let's discuss briefly some of the systemic problems in our society, and how they impact the subject of finances.

The Bible clearly teaches and expects that all adults are to be humble, hard working individuals, willing to accept whatever work we can get to support our families.[3] The only exception is for those with severely poor health. In our welfare culture, many people have come to expect that someone else will take care of them: the government, relatives, charities, etc. There are those who have preferred to live on welfare rather than work, and think they are clever in so doing. These are what the Bible calls *sluggards*, or just plain lazy people.[4] Biblically, laziness is a sin, and not to be condoned or reinforced by the congregation.[5]

WISE PLANNING

You should have a simple goal of building a savings account with enough to cover three months worth of expenses. Sooner or later rainy days do come. This goal should precede all plans for family trips, parties, presents, eating out, entertainment and other non-essential expenditures.[6]

DEBT EQUALS DEATH

Beware of debt.[7] See debt as death—it is a terrible burden on any family to be avoided at all costs. So make a committment to not go into debt, and if you *are* in debt, do all you can to get out of debt. Later in this chapter is a plan to help you break out of 'the debt trap.' It may sound strange, but we are to bring our expenses within our income level. Additionally, we need to wisely save for car maintenance, general medical needs, and so forth.

There are times when a helping hand is needed. Benevolence from any source is for help in *emergency situations*, not to help us maintain a middle class lifestyle. We are not to approach our congregation for assistance in paying our rent, *after* we foolishly spent our money on a vacation, a new wide-screen TV, or fashionable clothing items. More on this later, but for now, may the Lord help us to live as wise stewards, and to be content with the things He has blessed us with.

Breaking Out Of The Debt Trap

We live in a culture built on instant gratification—"buy now, pay later." There is one word you will never read in credit card applications—***Debt***. Synonyms of debt are: "to owe; to be obligated; to be liable; in default; destitute; needy; in difficulty; empty; having seen better days; unable to make ends meet." If they told you this to begin with, would you sign up? The bottom line is, debt is a trap. *"The borrower is enslaved to the lender."*[8] When you go into debt, you have lost your freedom.

Danger signs—entering the debt trap!
Living On Credit Instead Of Paying Cash

"Don't withhold repayment of your debts. Don't say 'some other time' if you can pay now."[9] If you have to live on credit, you are overspending. This reveals a lack of contentment, and presumes on future income. Using credit cards can make you more susceptible to impulse buying, and you will spend 25% more money when you shop than if you used cash!

Delaying Payment, Paying Minimum Payments

"Let no debt remain outstanding."[10] If you find yourself missing payments, making late

payments, paying the minimum due or withdrawing out of a reserve account, these are all red flags indicating you are spending more than you make.

UNABLE TO TITHE OR SAVE

"Will a man rob God? Yet you rob me. But you ask, 'How do we rob you?' In tithes and offerings."[11] *"The wise man saves for the future, but the foolish man spends whatever he gets."*[12] Tithing, giving 10% of our income to God's work and ministry, is a biblical norm.[13] This should be done graciously, not begrudgingly,[14] and out of an appreciation for the work of God being conducted both in our lives and around the world.[15] One way to look at it is not: how much of my money am I giving to God; but, how much of God's money am I spending on myself? Regarding saving for the future, if you're not saving any money, you're spending too much.

UNABLE TO PAY TAXES

Do you have money to pay your taxes? The Bible expects us to *"give unto Caesar that which is Caesar's"*[16] and *"Render to all what is due them: tax to whom tax is due."*[17] It's unrighteous to accept the benefits of our society without paying our fair share.

EXTRAVAGANT SPENDING

"Indulging in luxuries, wine, and food will never make you wealthy."[18] When you buy things just because you have the money or to impress others, you are headed straight into the debt trap. This is often motivated by "status-seeking."

Status has been explained as "buying things you don't need, with money you don't have, to impress people you may not even like!" True contentment is found not in things, but in the Lord, and what He can do for you and your family.[19] Living within your means is a testimony that His grace is your sufficiency.[20]

LOOKING FOR GET-RICH-QUICK IDEAS

"Steady plodding brings prosperity; hasty speculation brings poverty."[21] "Dreaming instead of doing is foolishness."[22] Those who are always looking for get-rich-quick schemes only prove that there's a sucker born every hour.

NINE STEPS OUT OF THE DEBT TRAP

1. COMMIT TO BECOMING DEBT FREE NOW!

"The wicked borrow and do not repay..."[23] Everything starts with a commitment. It's not going to be easy. It will take discipline, courage, delayed gratification, endurance, persistence, integrity, character and commitment to get out of debt. But with God, all things are possible.

2. FIRST THINGS FIRST

It's called the **"10-10-80 PLAN"**. Give to God 10%. Save 10%. Live on 80%. If you are 30 years old making $30,000 and follow this principle, at 55 you would have given $50,000 to God's work and saved $171,000. *"The purpose of tithing is to teach you always to put God first in your lives."*[24]

3. LIST ALL I OWN & ALL I OWE

"By wisdom a house is built, and through understanding it is established."[25] Get the facts.

List everything you owe, and to whom you owe it. Then list all of your possessions. (This is good for insurance purposes as well).

4. SELL! SELL! SELL!

You probably have some things you need to get rid of. Sell them out-right, or have a yard/garage sale. Then take the cash and pay down your debt. Yeshua taught that His disciples are to *"sell your possessions."*[26] Simply put, any possession that possesses you, sell it!

5. SET UP A REPAYMENT PLAN

"Good planning and hard work lead to prosperity."[27] You will never get out of debt without a plan. Get advice. Seek wise counsel.

6. REPAY IN HALF THE TIME

In deciding what you can repay in half the time, you may think this step is impossible. "You don't know how much I am in debt. I can't possibly double my payments." To this the Bible says, *"What is impossible with men is possible with God."*[28]

7. ADD NO NEW DEBT

If you use credit cards, pay them off every month, don't buy things not in your budget, and destroy any card if you go one month without paying it off. Here's the lesson: *"Be content with what you have."*[29]

8. SHARE YOUR PLAN WITH YOUR CREDITORS

Start with your smallest debt, and pay it off. Write a letter to your creditors telling them your plan. Ask for mercy. BE HONEST. *"When your ways please the Lord, He will make your enemies into friends."*[30]

9. STICK WITH IT!

"Let us not get tired of doing what is right, for after a while we will reap a harvest of blessing if we don't get discouraged and give up."[31] Getting out of debt can be a trying, arduous process. It will take some 'stick-to-a-tive-ness.' There will be times along the way where you won't feel that you are making progress, but you are. While little by little, you are chiseling away at your debt, little by little God is chiseling away on your personal character. You're growing, and your finances will reflect that fact! So be encouraged. Check your priorities, and know that God is for you!

And remember, the principles work, but you have to *work the principles*.

BENEVOLENCE: EMERGENCY RELIEF

If you find yourself in a financial crisis, you may be wondering if, and how, the Lord can help you. Well, He can, and does help us in this area of life. Generally God does this by helping you grow in wisdom using resources He's provided.

If you do have emergency money issues, many congregations provide benevolence. This *limited* amount is set aside to help for *emergency* needs, (i.e., "I'm bankrupt and they're shutting off my electricity," or "I lost my job I need food for my family," etc.) In these cases the congregation where you are a member in good standing will certainly want to help.

As stated earlier, benevolence is only *emergency aid*, not a financial convenience. In other words, benevolence is not there as a substitute for a lack of practical and biblical wisdom. If you do have an emergency and benevolence is needed, there may be procedures. These may include:

1. The *Shamashim* (Deacons) of the congregation are the ones to approach.[32] They may either have you fill out an application for benevolence or suggest some other option.

2. The *Shamashim* will probably evaluate the situation rather than make an immediate decision. In an obvious emergency situation they can probably act quickly. If approved, they make a request for the funds from the treasurer of the congregation.

3. If it is a large amount of money (over $250), the matter may be brought by the *Shamashim* before the *Zachanim* (Elders) or Governing Board for a decision. So, you may have to be both patient and willing to follow the procedures.

Before approaching our *spiritual* family for help, the Scriptures teach that we are to go to our *natural believing family* first (i.e., grandparents,parents, children, etc.)[33] Generally this is a one-time request, that may be expected to be repaid, or some work provided in exchange.[34]

The *Shamashim* may request to evaluate your full financial situation with you. There may be a member in your congregation who works as a financial adviser, and may graciously offer his or her services to the congregation.

This person may be asked to assist the *Shamashim* in these matters. Please speak with such a person if you need counsel in financial areas, as well as for employment counseling.

A Matter of Checks & Balances

You may be surprised to find that congregation leaders generally don't stick their noses into other peoples financial issues. Though they care very much, they counsel only when they are asked to help, unless there is a public problem that they need to deal with on behalf of the congregation. I actually believe that "minding my own business" is biblical.[35]

By the way, please understand that the congregation leader is not the kingpin who can dole out the money. The congregational leader, and *Zachanim* in general, oversee the work of the *Shamashim* and Trustees. With the *Shamashim* making the "benevolent" decsions, the congregation leader and *Zachanim* are free to deal with spiritual issues, and can bring correction if there is a problem.

Did you know?

Though they expect all members to tithe, congregation leaders are, and generally should be, unaware of an individual's giving to the congregation. This way congregation leaders can counsel purely on the basis of the spiritual issues, and not be influenced by how much or how little someone is giving.

PAT'S RECIPE
FOR
GETTING OUT OF DEBT!

1. Preheat oven to 425°
2. Place all credit cards on lightly greased cookie sheet.
3. Carefully place cookie sheet with credit cards in oven.
4. Bake until golden brown, or corners begin to turn up.
5. Carefully remove from oven, place on cooling rack.
6. Once sheet and cards have sufficiently cooled, slide cards off of sheet into garbage can.
7. Praise the Lord! Not only are you on your way out of the debt trap, but BAM!...this treat has NO calories!

(Recipe works with American Express, Diners Club, Discover, Master Card, Visa, various gas, store, and other charge cards.)

Apply these principles to your financial situation, and soon you'll be saying *"L'hit Raot", "See ya' later", "Adios", "Hasta la vista, baby"* to your debt problems!

QUESTIONS
FOR YOUR FURTHER STUDY AND CONSIDERATION

Are you presently tithing 10%, and saving 10% of your income? What decisions must you make to begin doing so?

What areas of financial weakness do you need to pray about and perhaps contact and discuss with a financial counselor? What keeps you from contacting this person?

Are you teaching your children biblically sound financial values by having them *earn* an allowance, rather than just giving them money? What other ways can you help your family understand the Bible's wisdom on finances?

FOOTNOTES

[1] See Psalm 24:1
[2] 2 Timothy 3:15
[3] Ecclesiastes 9:10
[4] Prov. 26:16
[5] see Prov. 6:6-11, 13:4, 20:4, 21:25, 22:13, 24:30-34, 1 Thess. 4:11,12; 2 Thess. 3:10-12 26:13-16
[6] Prov. 6:6-8
[7] See Proverbs 22:7
[8] Prov. 22:7
[9] Prov. 3:27,28, LB
[10] Romans 13:8, NIV
[11] Malachi 3:8, NIV
[12] Prov. 21:20, LB
[13] Matthew 23:23; Hebrews 7:4-10
[14] 2 Corinthians 9:7
[15] Gal. 6:6; 3 John 1:5-8
[16] Matthew 22:21
[17] Romans 13:7
[18] Prov. 21:17, GN
[19] Philippians 4:11-13
[20] 2 Corinthians 12:9
[21] Prov. 21:5, LB
[22] Ecclesiastes 5:7, LB
[23] Psalm 37:21, NIV
[24] Deut. 14:23, TLB
[25] Prov. 24:3
[26] Luke 12:33
[27] Proverbs 21:5, NLT
[28] Luke 18:27, NIV
[29] Hebrews 13:5, NIV
[30] Prov. 16:7, GN
[31] Galatians 6:9, LB
[32] Acts 6:1-6
[33] see 1 Tim. 5:4,8,16
[34] see 1 Tim. 5:10
[35] John 21:22

APPENDIX

Sometimes it's hard to formulate precisely what we believe, since the Bible contains so much information. The following are some key areas of *faith and practice* for all Messianic believers. Studying over these areas will give you further insight on our biblical faith in Messiah.

A MESSIANIC STATEMENT OF FAITH

1. **WE BELIEVE THERE IS ONE GOD, ETERNALLY EXISTENT IN THREE PERSONS** - Father, Son, and Ruach HaKodesh (Holy Spirit). We believe that God is all-knowing, all-powerful, ever-present, and changeless, and that He is holy, righteous, faithful, merciful and loving (Deut. 6:4; Isaiah 43:10,11; 48:16).

We believe that the Father is all the fullness of the Godhead invisible. We rejoice that He concerns Himself mercifully in the affairs of men, that He hears and answers prayer, and that He saves from sin and death all who come to Him through faith in Messiah Yeshua (Ex. 4:22; Matt. 3:17; John 1:12, 3:16; 8:24, 58; Gal. 3:26).

We believe that Messiah Yeshua is the eternal and only begotten Son of God, conceived of the Holy Spirit, born of a Jewish virgin, Miriam. He was sinless in His life and He made atonement for the sins of the world by the shedding of His blood unto death. We believe in His bodily resurrection from the dead, His ascension, His high priestly work in Heaven for us, and His visible premillenial return to the world according to His promise. (Leviticus 17:11; Psalm 22:16; 110:4; Isaiah 52:13-53:12; Daniel 9:26; Zechariah 12:10; Mark 10:45; Romans 3:24-26, 5:8,9;

2 Cor. 5:14, 21; 1 Peter 3:18; Isaiah 7:14, 9:6,7; Jer. 23:5,6; Micah 5:2; John 1:1, 8:58; 1 Tim. 3:16; Heb. 1:2,3; 1 Cor. 15:3-8; Heb. 7:1-25, 8: 1; 1 John 2:1).

We believe the Ruach HaKodesh (Holy Spirit) is a person of the Godhead; and as such, He possesses all the distinct attributes of Deity. He is ever present to glorify and testify of Messiah Yeshua. We believe that according to *Brit Chadasha* (New Covenant/New Testament), the Holy Spirit permanently indwells, regenerates, and seals the believer. He empowers, sovereignly imparting at least one spiritual gift to every believer for the purpose of edifying and equipping the Body of Messiah; guides, teaches, sanctifies, and fills believers; convicts the world of sin, righteousness, and judgment.

We believe the immersion of the Holy Spirit is both initiatory and universal. Believers should therefore seek to identify, utilize and develop their God-given gifts for service in the Lord (Gen. 1:2; Psalm 139:7,8; Neh. 9:20; 1 John 9:20; John 14:16,17, 15:26,27, 16:7-15; 1 Cor. 2:10,11, 12:4-31; 2 Cor. 13:14; Eph. 1:13,14, 4:30).

2. WE BELIEVE THAT THE BIBLE (OLD AND NEW COVENANTS) IS GOD'S COMPLETED WORD, that it was inerrantly written by divinely inspired men, that it is the supreme, infallible authority in all matters of faith and conduct, and that it is true in all that it affirms (Prov. 30:5,6; Isaiah 40:7,8; Jer. 31:31; Matt. 5:18; 2 Tim. 3:16; 2 Peter 1:21).

3. WE BELIEVE THAT BECAUSE OF THE ORIGINAL SIN OF ADAM, ALL PEOPLE ARE BY NATURE AND CHOICE SINFUL AND ALIENATED FROM GOD.

We believe that humanity was created in the image of God, but that humanity has no possible means of reconciling itself to God and that, by persisting in the sinful state of unbelief, man is justly condemned by God to eternal punishment. (Gen. 1:26,27, 2:17, 3:6; Is. 53:6, 64:6; Jer. 17:9; Mark 7:20-23; Jn. 2:24,25; Rom. 5:12-15; Eph. 2:1-3).

4. WE BELIEVE THAT MAN IS ONLY RECONCILED TO GOD—BEING JUSTIFIED BY GRACE THROUGH FAITH—IN THE ATONING WORK OF MESSIAH YESHUA. Being reconciled, man has peace with God and direct access to Him through Messiah Yeshua, and has the hope of eternal glory in Heaven with God. Furthermore, there is no way of salvation apart from faith in Messiah Yeshua for any person, Jewish or Gentile (Gen. 15:6; Habakkuk 2:4; John 1:12,13; 14:6; Acts 4:12; Romans 3:28; Eph. 1:7; 1 Tim. 2:5: Titus 3:5).

We believe that all who have truly trusted in Yeshua are kept eternally secure by the power of God through the new birth, the indwelling and sealing ministry of the Holy Spirit, and the intercession of Messiah Yeshua (John 10:28-30, 14:16,17; Romans 8:38-39; Eph. 4:30; 1 John 2:1; 1 Peter 1:23).

We believe that all who have trusted in Yeshua, though forgiven, still have to contend with the power of sin in this life. Each believer has the ability to choose sin or righteousness. God has made full provision for believers to live in obedience to Him through the complete atonement of Messiah Yeshua and the indwelling of the Spirit of God (John 17:17-19; Romans 6:1-11,7:15-25, 8:11-13; 1 John 1:8-2:2).

5. WE BELIEVE THE CONGREGATION IS A LIVING, SPIRITUAL BODY OF WHICH MESSIAH IS THE HEAD AND ALL TRUE BELIEVERS ARE MEMBERS.
The body of Messiah began at Shavuot (Pentecost) when believers were filled with the Holy Spirit after the ascension of Messiah Yeshua. It will be completed

when the Messiah returns for His bride. The body of Messiah is distinct from Israel and is composed of both Jewish and non-Jewish (Gentile) believers made into one new man by faith in Messiah Yeshua (Matt. 16:18; Acts 1:5, 2:14-38; 1 Cor. 12:13; Eph. 2:11-15, 5:23-27; Col. 1:18-20, 3:14,15).

We believe that the local congregation is an organized body of believers in Messiah Yeshua who have been through Mikvah/Tavilah (baptism) by immersion upon confession of faith and who associate for worship, fellowship, teaching, and service. We believe the local congregation is governed by its members through the Zakanim (Elders) and is not ruled by any outside political authority. Its purpose is to glorify God through worship, instruction, accountability, discipline, fellowship and outreach (Matt. 28:19,20; Acts 2:42-47; Eph. 4:11-13; Heb. 10:19-25). We believe Messiah commands Zicharon (the Lord's Supper) and believer's Mikvah (baptism) by immersion for observation by the Congregation (Matt. 28:18-20; Luke 22:19,20; 1 Cor. 11:23-26).

6. **WE BELIEVE THAT SATAN IS THE CHIEF ENEMY OF GOD AND OUR SOULS**, and that while he continues to rule this present world, Messiah's atoning death and resurrection have defeated him. Satan will suffer eternal punishment by being cast into the lake of fire after the Messiah's one thousand year Messianic reign (2 Cor. 4:4; Eph. 2:1-3; Col. 2:15; Rev. 20:10). Satan is the father of lies and anti-Semitism and hostility toward Israel. Believers can and should resist him and his demons by faith, applying Spiritual truth. We believe that though believers cannot be demon *possessed*, they can be demon *oppressed* (Genesis 3:1-19; Luke 10:18; John 8:44; Eph. 6:10-19; James 4:7,8; 1 Peter 5:8,9; Rev. 12:13).

We believe in the God-ordained ministry of holy angels to bring about God's intended plans and purposes and to minister to all believers (Isaiah 6:1-7; Daniel 10:10-21; Luke 15:10; Eph. 1:21; Heb. 1:14; Rev. 7:11,12).

7. WE BELIEVE THE PEOPLE OF ISRAEL, COMPRISED OF THE PHYSICAL DESCENDANTS OF ABRAHAM, ISAAC, AND JACOB, ARE CHOSEN BY GOD.

The Abrahamic Covenant expressed God's choice of Israel and His irrevocable, unconditional covenant to the Jewish people. Jewish believers have a unique two-fold identity as both the spiritual remnant of physical Israel and as members of the body of Messiah. Non-Jewish believers become adopted sons and daughters of Abraham and partakers of the spiritual blessings of Israel and are therefore grafted into the Jewish olive tree for service. We believe that it is the believer's duty and privilege to communicate the Good News of Messiah Yeshua to the Jewish people first, and also to the Gentiles, according to the Scriptures, in a clear yet sensitive way. It is also the believer's duty to support the God-given rights of Israel to the land while opposing anti-Semitism according to the provisions of the Abrahamic Covenant. We believe God has a special purpose and role for the nation of Israel and the Jewish people. We believe in the full physical and spiritual restoration of Israel at the Second Coming of the Messiah as proclaimed in the Scriptures (Gen. 12:1-3; 17:7,8, 26:3,4, 28:13-15; Exodus 19:6; Amos 3:2; 9:8; Zech. 12:10; 14:2-4; Matt. 23:39; John 4:22; Acts 3:19-21, 13:46; Rom. 1:16, 9:3-5; 10:1-5; 11:2-5, 23-26, 28-29; Eph. 2:14-19).

Believers are not under the authority of the Law of Moses (Torah), and therefore are not obligated to practice the Law of Moses. However, both Jewish and non-Jewish believers have the freedom in Messiah to enjoy those aspects of the Law of Moses (i.e., festivals, Shabbat) which are non-salvific (i.e., sacrifices) in light of New Covenant revelation. These aspects of the Law are not, nor ever were, a means of justification or sanctification, which are by grace through faith alone. For non-Jewish believers, such observances are a means of identifying with the Jewish community and expressing the Jewish roots of Biblical faith (Acts 21:24,25; Romans 6:14,15, 8:2-9, 10:4-9, 14:1-6; 1 Cor. 9:20,21; 2 Cor. 3:1-11; Gal. 3:3,11; Col. 2:16,17).

For more information on many of these subjects you can read *"Growing in Messiah: Vital Truths for Maturing Messianic Believers"* from Word of Messiah Ministries.

Prophecies of the Messiah

Subject	Old Covenant	New Covenant
A descendent of Abraham	Genesis 12:3	Matthew 1:1
From the tribe of Judah	Genesis 49:10	Luke 3:33
Heir of King David	Isaiah 9:7	Luke 1:32
He was to come before temple is destroyed	Malachi 3:1	Matthew 24:1
He was to be born in Bethlehem	Micah 5:2(1)	Luke 2:4-7
He was to have a Galilean ministry	Isaiah 9:1 (Isaiah 8:23)	Matthew 4:13-16
He was to be born of a virgin	Isaiah 7:14	Luke 1:26,27,30
He is the Son of God	Psalm 2:7, 12	Matthew 3:17
He is God in the flesh (Mighty God)	Isaiah 9:6(5); 10:21	Hebrews 1:8-12
A forerunner was to proceed Him	Malachi 3:1	Luke 7:24
He was to be initially rejected by Israel	Isaiah 53:3	John 1:11
He was to die as an atonement for our sins	Isaiah 53:6,8,11,12	Matthew 20:28
He would be resurrected	Psalm 16:10	Luke 24:6,7
He will one day be accepted by Israel	Zechariah 12:10	Revelation 1:7; 7:4; 14:1-4

Redemption In

God's Work	Feast		Leviticus 23	Month
Gaining His People		Passover	4-5	Nisan 1ST MONTH
		Unleavened Bread	6-8	Nisan 1ST MONTH
		First Fruits	9-14	Nisan 1ST MONTH
Grounding His People		Shavuot, Weeks or Pentecost	15-21	Sivan 3RD MONTH
		...Work In the Fields...	22	Summer Months
Gathering His People		Trumpets ("New Year")	23-25	Tishrei 7TH MONTH
		Day of Atonement	28-32	Tishrei 7TH MONTH
		Tabernacles or Booths	33-44	Tishrei 7TH MONTH

The Feasts of Israel

Meaning	Fulfillment	God's Result
Ransom of Soul	1 Corinthians 5:7	Salvation
Removal of Sin	1 Corinthians 5:8	
Resurrection of Savior	1 Corinthians 15:21-23	
Redeemed Body	James 1:18 Acts 2:1-10	Sanctification
Reaching and Reaping	Matthew 28:18-20 Acts 1:8	
Rapture of the Body of Messiah	1 Corinthians 15:52 1 Thessalonians 4:16,17	Glorification
Regeneration of Israel	Zechariah 12:10-13:1 Matthew 23:39	
Reign of Messiah	Zechariah 14:16 Revelation 7:9,15	

BLESSINGS FOR YOUR HOME AT SHABBAT

Here are some blessings we have said around our table each Friday evening at meal time. Blessings over the Shabbat candles by the woman of the house begin the meal; her head is covered with a scarf to signify reverence and humility before the Lord. With the house lights dimmed, two (or three candles) are lit by the honored woman, who circles the lights three times with her hands, drawing in the light. She then recites the blessing, which is spoken or chanted in Hebrew, and repeated in English. Her eyes may be covered with her hands as a further symbol of reverence for the Lord. At the end of the prayer, she makes eye contact with the family and greets them with "Shabbat Shalom," which means "Sabbath Peace", and the family members greet one another with "Shabbat Shalom."

A Messianic Shabbat candle lighting prayer

Ba-rooch ah-ta Adonai,
El-lo-hay-noo meh-lech ha-oh-lahm,
as-sher keed-sha-noo
beed-va-reh-kha v'na-than la-noo et
Yeshua m'she-khay-noo,
v'tzee-va-noo l'he-oat oar la-oh-lahm. Amen.

Blessed are You, O Lord our God,
King of the Universe,
Who has sanctified us in Your Word,
and given us Yeshua our Messiah,
and commanded us to be light to the world. Amen.

Traditional Shabbat candle lighting prayer

Baruch Atah Adonai,
Elohaynu Melech Ha-olam,

*Asher kid'shanu B'Mitzvotav
V'tzivanu l'hadliyk ner shel Shabbat.*

*"Blessed are You, O Lord our God,
King of Universe,
Who has sanctified us in Your commandments,
and has commanded us
to kindle the Sabbath lights."
Amen.*

Next, the head of the house breaks off a piece of bread from the challah loaf, (in some homes the bread is distributed to all) then says a blessing over it:

*Ba-rooch ah-ta Adonai,
El-lo-hay-noo meh-lech ha-oh-lahm
ha mot-zi lechem meen ha aretz. Omen.*

*Blessed are You, O Lord our God
King of the Universe
who brings forth bread from the ground. Amen*

Then, as all lift their cups, the head of the house says this blessing over the wine or grape juice:

*Ba-rooch ah-ta Adonai,
El-lo-hay-noo meh-lech ha-oh-lahm,
bo-ray po-ree ha ga-fen. Omen*

*Blessed art thou O Lord
Our God King of the Universe
Who creates the fruit of the vine. Amen.*

All partake of their cups wishing each other "Shabbat Tov," or "Shabbat Shalom"—a good Sabbath, or Sabbath peace.

There are other blessings as well, but these are the most commonly recited.[2] In a Messianic home, it is also good to pray with thanksgiving *"in the Name of Yeshua the Messiah our Lord"*—*"B'Shem Yeshua HaMashiach Adoneinu."*

BE SPIRITUALLY SENSITIVE TO YOUR JEWISH FAMILY & FRIENDS

When discussing Yeshua and spiritual issues, some care must be taken so that your Jewish family and friends will hear what you *are* saying, rather than what you are *not* saying. Because of anti-Semitism in 'Church history', many Jewish people think that to believe in Yeshua is also to renounce one's own Jewish identity, Jewish heritage, betray Holocaust victims and survivors, etc. Below is a simple chart from WMM's book *"Even you can Share the Jewish Messiah!"* to help clarify these issues.

I hope you find this helpful in communicating the Good New to those whom you love most.

DON'T SAY	DO SAY
CHRIST	MESSIAH
CHRISTIAN	BELIEVER IN YESHUA/JESUS
'CONVERTED' JEW	MESSIANIC JEW
CHURCH	CONGREGATION
CROSS	MESSIAH'S DEATH
TRINITY	TRI-UNITY OR TRIUNE NATURE
SALVATION/JUSTIFICATION	ATONEMENT/FORGIVENESS
OLD TESTAMENT	HEBREW SCRIPTURES
NEW TESTAMENT	NEW COVENANT

A Simple Prayer of Faith

Perhaps through this book you have come to see your need for Messiah in your life. If you have come to recognize your need for forgiveness and want to trust in Yeshua as your Messiah, you can receive His forgiveness for your sins, and enter into a new relationship with God, and receive eternal life right now.

This simple prayer can help to focus your thoughts on God and express your heart by trusting in Yeshua for salvation.

"Dear God, I'm sorry for my sins and ask for your forgiveness of all my sins through the atonement in Yeshua the Messiah. Thank you for loving me and saving me forever...

...in Messiah's Name. Amen"

If you *sincerely* prayed this prayer of faith, **Mazel Tov!** You are now a child of God by faith in Yeshua!

We, at Word of Messiah Ministries, would love to hear from you and rejoice with you for what God has done in your life! Please let us know if we can be of any help to you as you grow in the Lord and your understanding of Messiah.

Welcome to the family, and Shalom!

Other Books & Materials by WMM

1. The Feasts of Israel - Eye-opening! The meaning of Israel's Feasts in light of the New Covenant: *Passover, Rosh Hashana, Yom Kippur, Sukkot, Hanukkah, more!* (232 pp.)

2. The Messianic Answer Book - Answers to the 14 most asked questions Jewish people have about the faith. Excellent tool for sharing with those seeking 'The Answer'! (110 pp.)

3. Messianic Life Lessons from the Book of Jonah - The book of Jonah reveals a Holy, Almighty God who loves people desperately, and will go to any lengths, or depths to reach lost and sinful people. This book will help you to understand God's purpose and plan for your life and rather then flee His will, you may fulfill it! (150pp.)

4. Messianic Life Lessons from the Book of Ruth - The book of Ruth is a vivid illustration of the teachings in the book of Romans on salvation by grace, the necessity of faith, and God's eternal plan for Israel, all pictured in one Gentile believer who believed the God of Israel would have her reach out to a lost sheep of the house of Israel. (320 pp.)

5. Following Yeshua: Foundational Discipleship for Messianic Believers - Develop a solid foundation by learning basic truths needed to grow in God's love. (65 pp.)

6. Growing in Messiah: Vital Truths for Maturing Messianic Believers - Answers to challenging questions facing Jewish and non-Jewish believers in Yeshua. Can be used as a follow-up to *Following Yeshua*. (123 pp.)

7. Even You Can Share The Jewish Messiah! - Learn how to share your faith with Jewish people in a sensitive, yet effective manner. "Do's & Do Not's", history of 'the Church' & the Jews, Messianic Prophecy chart, and more…(27 pp.)

8. The Messianic Passover Haggadah - The perfect guide for conducting your own Passover Seder, for family or congregational use, or to simply learn more about Passover. (40 pp.)

9. Sense & Sensibility - Honoring God With My Life –In this expositional study of Titus 2:3-5 you will discover how to live a life according to God's calling and His design. (232pp.)

Additional Helpful Resources

"Messianic Jewish Identity"
"Your Home-Front Testimony"
"Dealing with Death in the Family"
    God's Appointed Customs—Barney Kasdan

"Confessing the Faith"
    Betrayed—Stan Telchin
    Jesus was a Jew—Armold Fruchtenbaum
    What the Rabbis know about the Messiah
                        —Rachmiel Frydland

"Celebrating the Jewish Holidays"
    God's Prophetic Calendar—Lehman Strauss
    God's Appointed Times—Barney Kasdan
    A Family Guide to the Biblical Holidays
                    —Robin Scarlata, Linda Pierce

"Messianic Marriage Matters"
    Joined Together (Video)—Chosen People Ministries
    The Marriage Builder—Larry Crabb
    I Kissed Dating Goodbye—Joshua Harris
    Passion & Purity—Elisabeth Elliot

"Your Faith & Your Finances"
    Debt-Free Living—Larry Burkett

Recommended Reading
    Israelology—Arnold Fruchtenbaum
    Our Jewish Friends—Louis Goldberg
    The Life & Times of Jesus The Messiah
                        —Alfred Edersheim
    Are There Two Ways of Atonement
                        —Louis Goldberg

FOR MORE INFORMATION,
PLEASE CALL OR WRITE:

WORD OF MESSIAH MINISTRIES
P.O. BOX 79238
CHARLOTTE, NC
28271, USA

PHONE/FAX: 704-455-1948

VISIT OUR WEBSITE AT:

WWW.WORDOFMESSIAH.ORG

Copyright © 2003, Sam Nadler, Word of Messiah Ministries
All rights reserved.

Notes

Made in the USA
Monee, IL
24 October 2020